RAP MUSIC
HAD A
CONSCIENCE

WHEN

RAP MUSIC
HAD A
CONSCIENCE

The Artists, Organizations, and Historic Events
that Inspired and Influenced the "Golden Age"
of Hip-Hop from 1987 to 1996

TAYANNAH LEE McQUILLAR

Foreword by Brother J of X Clan

Thunder's Mouth Press
New York

WHEN RAP MUSIC HAD A CONSCIENCE
The Artists, Organizations, and Historic Events that Inspired and Influenced the "Golden Age" of Hip-Hop from 1987 to 1996

Published by
Thunder's Mouth Press
An Imprint of Avalon Publishing Group, Inc.
245 West 17th Street, 11th Floor
New York, NY 10011

Copyright © 2007 by Tayannah Lee McQuillar

First Printing, April 2007

Library of Congress Cataloging-in-Publication Data is available.

ISBN-10: 1-56025-919-1
ISBN-13: 978-1-56025-919-0

9 8 7 6 5 4 3 2 1

Interior design by *Ivelisse Robles Marrero*

Printed in the United States of America
Distributed by Publishers Group West

Contents

Foreword
by Brother J of X-Clan

Peace!

I am known as the Grand Verbalizer Funkin-lesson Brother J, vocalist for the pioneer hip-hop group known as the X-Clan.

The late Lumumba Carson (Professor X) and Claude Gray (the Architect Paradise) were the elder portion of the X-Clan. We were one of the first groups that walked with our mentors on stage, at interviews, etc. This was the first symbol of maturity that X-Clan offered to hip-hop culture: respect your elders.

Lumumba Carson (before evolving into Professor X) was a NYC show promoter and artist manager. He worked with icon artists like Just-Ice, Big Daddy Kane, Positive K, and Stetsasonic.

Brother Claude Gray was down with the management team of the New York hip-hop hotspot Latin Quarter and he was responsible for getting the majority of hip-hop's veterans their first exposure and payment for performance.

It was up to me and DJ Suga Shaft to join Carson and Gray by stepping up to the plate and represent the voice of our generation through rhythmic poetry and turntabalism.

A bonus to this divine mesh was that Bro. Carson was the founder of a youth organization known as the BlackWatch Movement. The BlackWatch Movement was a Black Nationalist movement and think tank for youth who sought alliance to something active and hip. Black Nationalism was not being taught as a negative aspect, it was more like passing on the knowledge of why oppression continues to follow people of color.

I am a native New Yorker, born and raised in Brooklyn. I consider the five boroughs the Mesopotamia of hip-hop, the original elements of the griot and the djembe evolved to the two turntables and a microphone. I was a seventeen-year-old soldier when I started in the rap music business. The Creator put me in the seat to "verbalize" the expression of elders and the frustrations of the youth. The BlackWatch Movement grew without any media coverage—that let me know that we were doing the right thing.

The music became a tool to expand our voice as activists, from the streets of Brooklyn to the world. Our first responsibility was to our generation and to our people. The music and the rapping came second.

Being an artist back in the day was an honor because there weren't that many rap artists signed to major labels. 4th & Broadway/Island records was bold enough to expose something new to hip-hop.

The pressure from the street was to avoid crossover. Nobody in my hood listened to those Bobby Brown rappers. Then block party lyricism started taking the backseat to jingle rap and sex appeal. How could we stay raw and still make money for the record label? That was another challenge.

I think Eric B. & Rakim and Big Daddy Kane were able to satisfy the consumer base by remaining knowledgeable and satisfy the record company by staying paid in full. It is a very hard thing to do.

I've been asked if I think that Black Nationalism will become popular again. Black Nationalism should not be measured in that way. It is a tool of the people.

The music of Black Nationalism is another story. Will there be another James Brown, Curtis Mayfield, or Nina Simone? Yes. Black Nationalism exists because the rights of indigenous people are being violated. As long as that is the case, other artists will rise in musical protest. The music of Black Nationalism reflects the counteraction, not the reaction.

The greatest gift that hip-hop has given to the world is power to use the freedom of speech as a weapon. The problem with wanna-be rappers is that they want to be executives from day one. They don't understand the concepts of protocol and dues paying. A recording label wants to invest in a true hustler. Corporations can't sell what doesn't work. If they feel that you have ability but then you don't manifest the potential, they have to mold you into a marketable product. If you spend some time paying your dues, then you will have a following before a record label signs you. Then, you can't be molded to someone else's vision.

If conscious artists want to create business with music machines (major or independent), they have to be able to prove that they can sell units. Period! These are our streets and we can dictate what goes down on the listener side and the creative side. It is all about dues paying.

I salute all of the artists of today who keep the art of conscious hip-hop alive.

No sellout.

No Retreat.

Peace and prosperity,
Brother J

Introduction

It is a dreary gray afternoon on March 17, 2006, as I nervously wait outside of the Antioch Baptist Church in Brooklyn to attend the funeral of Robert

"Lumumba" Carson also known as Professor X, the Overseer of X-Clan.

The church is located on a residential street that is amazingly quiet in comparison to the hustle and bustle of Kosciusko Street where I got off the J train. Lined with refurbished brownstones and townhouses, it appears far removed from the deteriorated world just four blocks away.

As I await the beginning of the service, I watch groups of mourners clad in bright Afrocentric garb with shiny gold ankhs, sisters with locked hair and floor-sweeping skirts, a few bow-tied brothers from the Nation of Islam, and a host of Five Percenters and Zulus who could not necessarily be determined by their dress but by their unique way of communicating.

I know the service won't be a traditional one since the departed abhorred conformity, but I'm wearing a classic funeral uniform consisting of a black suit and oversized dark shades. Since I have never met Robert Lumumba Carson, it is impossible for me to really mourn him. So, why am I so sad? The answer is simple: His alter ego Professor X was one of the symbols of my adolescence and of a time when rap artists were unafraid to "take it to the man."

As the people begin filing into the church, I notice two teenage girls giddily walking down the street. I stop them and ask if they ever heard of X-Clan. Their faces contort and they shake their heads as they stare at an African staff-carrying elder in the background. They ask me who the X-Clan were. I tell them. One of the girls snaps her fingers and says, "I never heard of X-Clan but I know about that positive shit. My brother listens to other groups that rap that stuff but I don't. When I get home, I wanna chill . . . not get all riled up or whatever."

Her friend nods in agreement and the two girls walk away without looking back. They have summed up the attitude of the majority of contemporary urban youth about conscious hip-hop: the reluctance to reflect on the broader world around them, the obsession with nonaction (except when it comes to partying), and a fierce determination not to deal with the past.

I was born in 1977, so the soundtrack of my early childhood consists of pop acts like Michael Jackson,

Prince, Madonna, and Culture Club. Rock bands like Guns N' Roses, Aerosmith, U2, and INXS. R&B artists like New Edition, Guy, Al B. Sure!, and Whitney Houston. Lesser appreciated bohemian acts from abroad like Neneh Cherry and Terence Trent D'Arby and rappers like Run-D.M.C., LL Cool J, MC Lyte, Salt-N-Pepa, and Big Daddy Kane.

Then came adolescence with its uncertainty, fear, and anger. The conscious rappers appeared just then with a brand-new musical sound that fit my mood perfectly. It was those literate, multidimensional, "Insight produces Incite" politically-charged brothers and sisters whose music sparked my curiosity about Black history, social injustice, and true multiculturalism.

When Rap Music Had a Conscience is the story of how a group of talented, idealistic, confrontational, prismatic, and educated (self or institutionally) youth examined the world around them and not only reported their findings on wax but also explored *why* things were the way they were in their community and what could be done to correct the downside.

It is also a look back at certain politically-charged

events, literature, and movies that affected these artists.

I hope that this book will reignite interest in and create a dialogue about this part of rap music history.

Peace,
Tayannah Lee McQuillar

Hip hop is a cultural form that attempts to negotiate the experience of marginalization, brutally truncated opportunity, and oppression within the cultural imperatives of African American and Caribbean history, identify and community.

—Tricia Rose, Professor of Africana Studies at Brown University

1

The True Def Poets

The first recorded rap song was a party tune called "Rapper's Delight," which was released in 1979. Over the next few years, rap music continued to focus on moving the crowd to dance. Then along came the conscious rappers who did not push the party rappers out. The groups simply coexisted and did their own thing in the marketplace. Both types of rap music were shunted to the side when the gangsta rap era began but that is another story altogether. This book is a celebration of the conscious era.

What is conscious rap music? Songs that are responsible, thought provoking, and/or inspirational toward positive change or a cry of protest against social injustice.

In the mainstream, music with serious sociopolitical commentary didn't become the norm until the sixties but it existed in the Black community since the first Africans arrived on the shores of the Americas.

From Negro spirituals sung by the enslaved people encouraging escape with songs like "Wade in the Water" to jazz master John Coltrane's requiem "Alabama" written in response to the racist bombing of the 16th Street Baptist Church to James Brown's Black Power Movement anthem "Say it Loud! (I'm Black and I'm Proud)," African Americans have always used music to express opposition to the staggering burdens that weighed them down.

Historically, the delivery of the message fluctuated with the political mood of the country. During slavery and periods of conservative extremes, protest music has been heavily coded out of fear of white scrutiny and/or punishment, and during a liberal climate the message is more overt.

However, conscious hip-hop doesn't only include hard-core politically-minded artists or protest music. It includes a range of styles and philosophies from jazz-rap fusion to bohemian "peace and love" and everything in between.

It is important to note that the very existence of hip-hop culture is "conscious" as it gives a voice to the most marginalized segments of our population who would otherwise have none. Poor Black youth, with no representation in the mainstream media via magazines like *Seventeen* or television shows like *Saved by the Bell* or *Beverly Hills, 90210*, created hip-hop culture using fashion, graffiti art, and a type of music called rap.

Thus, the hip-hop culture once again affirms the

truth of the old saying that necessity is the mother of invention.

Rap music developed during the economic devastation and subhuman living conditions of the Reagan years (1981–1989). Ronald Reagan started his bid for the presidency by talking about states' rights at the Neshoba County Fair in Mississippi. The phrase "states' rights" started before the Civil War when slaveholders used it to affirm their right to own other human beings. It made a comeback among white racists when Martin Luther King Jr. was trying to stamp out segregation in the 1960s, and Reagan used it in his speeches to gain right-wing supporters.

On another occasion Reagan was speaking in front of an all-white crowd in Stone Mountain, Georgia, and delighted the crowd when he declared that Jefferson Davis was one of his heroes.

After winning the election and gaining the White House, Reagan (who supported apartheid in South Africa) proceeded to slash or discontinue many American social programs that benefited children, the poor, and the elderly. Suddenly, busing programs were blocked, funds for the Head Start program became almost nonexistent, budgets for free school lunch programs were slashed, financial aid for poor college students was cut, prisons were built, and the unemployment rate soared.

In spite of these conditions, many old school rap artists simply did not address the despair in their communities. Instead they mostly concentrated on competitive verbal gymnastics and a call-and-response system in order to rock the party. The call-and-response techniques are a form of spontaneous verbal and nonverbal interaction between speaker and listener in which all of the statements ("calls") are punctuated by expressions ("responses") from the listener. It is common in West African cultures. It wasn't until 1982 with Grandmaster Flash and the Furious Five's "The Message" that the harsh realities of ghetto life were put to a hip-hop beat. Raw and full of a passion that only a person who lived what they spoke could have, Flash and his crew explained the depressed environment that they grew up in and the toll it took on the spirit and minds of the people. Revolutionary and danceable, the single caught everyone's attention—from the slums of the South Bronx to the clubs of

Greenwich Village. It was Grandmaster Flash and the Furious Five's innovation that would inspire a new generation of MCs to put contemporary issues on wax on a consistent basis.

Triumph and Punishment

During the eighties the rich got richer and the poor got poorer, unemployment was high, and racial tensions were even higher. People of color were angry and the spirit of protest hung thick in the air. Armed with lessons learned from their parents' and grandparents' era when southern African Americans inspired millions of red, brown, and yellow people all over the world to rebel against oppression, Black students and their supporters once again took to the streets.

Their main focus was the termination of apartheid in South Africa, but the consciousness from that struggle made people of color more aware of continuing injustices at home. It was because of their efforts that Congress eventually passed the comprehensive Anti-Apartheid Act of 1986, and Africana, Latino, Asian, and Women's Studies

Departments that had only existed on very few college campuses became the norm.

It wasn't only the college students who were making some political noise in the Black community; there were other organizations like the Nation of Gods and Earths (commonly known as the Five Percenters) that were inspiring youth to embrace positive change and self-reflection as a means to at least get out of the ghetto mentally until they could physically get out of the ghetto itself.

Then crack (cocaine mixed with water and baking soda, then heated to a rocklike density) entered the Black community in 1983 and silenced the protestors just like a wave of heroin (along with an FBI initiative called Cointelpro) had ended the Black Power Movement a decade earlier.

The following conscious rappers stepped in to fill the void:

Afrika Bambaataa

During his early teenage years Kevin Donovan was a member of a street gang called the Black Spades. A visit to Africa changed his life. When he returned to

America, he changed his name to Afrika Bambaataa and started the Zulu Nation. He started his hip-hop life as a DJ and producer before becoming a vocalist. Uncompromisingly Afrocentric and committed to community activism, Bambaataa has released over a dozen albums, including: *Planet Rock: The Album* (1986), *1990–2000: The Decade of Darkness* (1991), *Zulu War Chant* (1993), and *Lost Generation* (1996). In 1990, *Life* magazine named Bambaataa one of the most important Americans of the twentieth century.

Arrested Development

Todd Thomas aka Speech and Timothy Barnwell aka Headliner created this group while both were living in Atlanta, Georgia. Their first album (which won a Grammy Award) was called *3 Years, 5 Months and 2 Days in the Life Of . . .* because it took that long for them to get a record deal.

Their music was political but it had a soft, rhythmic sound that soothed the soul while Speech fed the mind.

"People Everyday" is a conversation with the Lord—asking for help in understanding injustice and reminiscing about the forefathers. "Tennessee" explains that Speech is searching for a new religion as the Baptists ask poor folk to suffer through their plight and wait for the pearly gates of heaven to open up. "Mr. Wendel" is a song about the plight of a homeless man names Mr. Wendel. Through this tune, Arrested Development tried to teach the public that just because a person doesn't have a place to live and may appear disheveled, it doesn't mean they are a "bum." Everyone has a story.

Spike Lee approached the group in the early 1990s and asked them to create a song to be used in his upcoming film about the life of Malcolm X. The result was the wildly popular "Revolution."

The group disbanded in 1996 and Speech went solo.

Brand Nubian

This New Rochelle (a suburb of New York) group formed in 1989 and was composed of Maxwell Dixon aka Grand Puba, Derek Murphy aka Sadat X, and Lorenz DeChalus aka Lord Jamar. Everything was on point about Brand Nubian. They had two fine brothers in the group (Derek X and Lord Jamar), they were conscious, and the beats by DJ Alamo were slammin'. Listening to their songs was like learning something from an older brother or a trusted family friend. Brand Nubian gave me and a lot of my friends the impression that all Five Percenters were completely trutstworty and honest people, which, of course, isn't true about any group. On "Slow Down," they pleaded with young Black women to wait before becoming sexually active and use the free time to get an education. On "Love vs. Hate," they pointed out that self-hate was a bigger killer of Black people than crack or the police.

The group became controversial when they recorded "Drop the Bomb," a tune that used the word "devil" when referring to Caucasians. It was a song that made many white people very angry. Even some employees in the marketing department at the record company (Elecktra) that they were signed to, rose up and accused them of reverse racism.

They kept going and their followers kept buying their albums. The group didn't break up or see a drop in sales until years later when Grand Puba decided to go solo.

De La Soul

Three high school classmates from Long Island formed this group during the late 1980s. They were

Kelvin Mercer aka Posdonuous, David Jude Joli-
coeur aka Trugoy the Dove, and Vincent Mason aka
Pasemaster Mase. Like most musicians, the young
men knocked on a lot of doors in their struggle to
get a record deal. Their luck changed when Prince
Paul (leader of the rap group called Stetsasonic)
heard their tape and convinced a music executive at
Tommy Boy Records to give them a contract. Their
songs never alluded to any particular religion, philosophy, or political agenda. They emphasized
self-reliance, perseverance, and responsible (non-
promiscuous) sexual activity

Their first album, *3 Feet High and Rising,* was
released in 1989. It was funny, clever, and solid in
that every song has an important message to
deliver.

"Stakes Is High" was a scathing and highly critical
indictment of the gangster lifestyle. "Me, Myself and
I" stressed the importance of self-definition. "Say No
Go" encouraged young people to avoid drug use.

Eric B. & Rakim

There are as many opinions about rappers and rap
music as there are stars in the sky. But everyone (from

journalists to producers to rappers who have reached the heights of international superstardom) who truly understands the art of rapping agrees that Rakim is the greatest MC to ever pick up a microphone. When it comes to rhyming, verbal dexterity, and sheer flow, he has no peer. So far, no rapper has ever even come close.

Eric Barrier aka Eric B. and William Griffin Jr. aka Rakim met in the mid-1980s at a party where Eric Barrier was working as a DJ and showing off his considerable turntable skills. Although they enjoyed huge success with big party hits like "I Ain't No Joke," "Eric B is President," and "I Know You Got Soul," they also made a point of doing socially conscious songs.

"Casualties of War" delivered vignettes about the horrors of battlefields like Vietnam, and "Teach the Children" is a staccato cry for help with issues like discrimination and drug abuse.

The duo made dozens of hit singles and Rakim always had something meaningful to say. Sure I heard rhymes like "I'm God, G is the 7th letter made" and that made me think but it didn't matter what Rakim was rapping about. He could recite the alphabet and make it sound dope.

Gangstarr

DJ Premier and MC Guru burst on the scene in the early '90s. Guru's laid-back monotone, storytelling skills, and mature demeanor made him seem older than his years. This MC didn't go easy on anyone. He held everyone up to scrutiny and called it as he saw it with Premier's jazzy beatmaking keeping score in the background.

"Execution of a Chump" talks about the Black snakes who pretend to be activists but who are simply exploiters of their own community. "Who's Gonna Take the Weight" pleads for the folks to take personal responsibility for their actions, and "Stay Tuned" reminds us all that our forefathers worked hard for our freedom and every time a Black body falls to gunfire, their work seems to be in vain.

Time and again, Gangstarr was urged by the music industry executives to make their records just a little more commercial. Each time, Premier and Guru said no. They had no interest in crossing over and pleasing folks from other cultures. It was enough that Black folks loved them.

Grandmaster Flash & the Furious Five

This quintet unwittingly took rap music from the party to the protest. The group was composed of Joseph Saddler aka Grandmaster Flash, Melvin Glover aka Melle Mel, Keith Wiggins aka Cowboy, Nathaniel Glover aka Kid Creole, Eddie Morris aka Mr. Ness, and Guy Williams aka Rahiem. They became famous very fast in 1982 with a song called "The Message" because of Flash's unrivaled cutting and scratching skills combined with Melle Mel's scorching and fear-filled stories, which introduced the world to life in the crumbling tenements of the South Bronx ghetto. The chorus, that went: "So don't push me cuz I'm close to the edge, I'm tryin' not to lose my head . . . It's like a jungle sometimes it makes me wonder how I keep from goin' under" spoke to every poverty-stricken, desperate, angry, and terrified teenager in America and then reached overseas. "White Lines," an anticocaine song, warned, begged, and pleaded for those who loved the white powder to put the coke spoon down.

Ice Cube

It was a total shock when Cube (born O'Shea Jackson) jumped on the conscious rap bandwagon with an album called *Death Certificate*. After all, this was the man who practically invented the celebration of thuggery most commonly known as gangsta rap. What happened? Did he have a religious conversion? Did he have an Ebenezer Scrooge–like experience wherein three ghosts showed up to point out the error of his ways?

We may never know.

Death Certificate is one of the rawest examples of just how hard-core political rap could become.

"A Bird in the Hand" tells the tale of a young Black man's struggle to survive by working low-paying jobs that don't provide enough money to take care of his family. He speaks bitterly about the lack of resources available to him. The song disses the Bush administration (George H.W. Bush) for not providing equal opportunities or programs to improve his life circumstances. "Stay True to the Game" is a song about African American sellouts who imitate whites and do anything to separate themselves from other Black people. "Look Who's Burnin'" is a cautionary tune aimed at promiscuous men who don't wear condoms and end up contracting sexually transmitted diseases.

It was good for Black boys who once emulated

Ice Cube's gangsta stance to see him turn around and behave more responsibly.

Jeru the Damaja

Kendrick Jeru Davis aka Jeru the Damaja started writing his own rap lyrics at the age of ten. He befriended DJ Premiere and Guru during the late 1980s and they recognized the genius of his hard-core conscious style. He became their protégé and they let him rhyme on "I'm the Man," one of the singles on Gangstarr's *Daily Operations* album.

In 1994, Jeru released his first album, *The Sun Also Rises in the East*. It berated gangsters, commercially focused rappers, parents who don't give their children proper guidance, and the various forms of mental enslavement used to keep poor people from rising up to confront the rich who live off them. The album is considered a classic. He went on to release three more albums, *Wrath of the Math* (1996), *Heroz4Hire* (1999), and *Divine Design* (2003).

KRS-One

Kris Parker aka KRS-One kicked rhymes that were so socially conscious and drop-dead political that some folks on the street nicknamed him The Teacher as an ultimate sign of respect. What is interesting about KRS-One is that he started off as a hard-core rapper, talking about crime and thugging. He was a high school dropout who spent most of his time living in homeless shelters. Then he and Scott Sterling, the social worker assigned to his case, became good friends. Like Parker, Sterling also had an interest in the rap game and performed as a DJ in his spare time under the name Scott La Rock. The two became a rap group called Boogie Down Productions and their songs, that sometimes celebrated street life, earned them a large following.

Then Scott was shot to death while trying to break up an argument between two young people and a devastated KRS-One became a solo act and one of the most socially conscious rappers of the era. He had learned the hard way that gunfire was nothing to celebrate.

His first solo album, *By All Means Necessary,* is a self-consciously Malcolm X–inspired imaging of hip-hop and its potential as a force for Black self-determination. Later KRS-One used some of the

Afrocentric perspectives of Yosef A.A. ben-Jochannan (former Cornell University professor and author of *Black Man of the Nile and His Family*) in his anthem "You Must Learn." He argued for the teaching of Afrocentric history and provided in a video positive depictions of Blacks, including Black biblical figures such as Moses.

He founded the Stop the Violence Movement and released his signature song, "Self- Destruction." In 1989, The Teacher gave $500,000 from the sale of "Self-Destruction" to the National Urban League.

Mos Def

Dante Terrell Smith aka Mos Def is a native New Yorker and a Muslim. He worked with De La Soul before releasing his first solo album, *Black on Both Sides* (1999). An artist who tells it like it is and calls it like he sees it, Mos Def has put out lyrics that warn rap music fans that corporate white men "is runnin' this rap shit," and corporations like MTV, Viacom, AOL, and Time Warner are the real forces in Black music and that Black rappers have little to no power in the whole game. His other solo albums include *The New Danger* (2004) and *Tru3Magic* (2006). He is also famous for hosting Def Comedy Jam.

Nas

Nasir bin Olu Dara Jones aka Nas is a native New Yorker who decided on a career in hip-hop before he was thirteen years old. He started out calling himself Nasty Nas and got his first break as a guest act on an album by Main Source. After a few more years of struggle, Nas found a manager with some clout and Columbia Records picked him up. His debut album, *Illmatic* (which was produced by Q-Tip, DJ Premier, and Pete Rock), was released in 1994 and eventually went platinum. It is considered one of the best albums in rap music history. His other solo albums include: *It was Written, I Am, Nastradamus,* and *Stillmatic.*

Paris

Oscar Jackson Jr. aka Paris is a San Francisco native who burst on the rap music scene after earning a degree in economics from the University of

California-Davis. The video for his first single, *The Devil Made Me Do It*, was banned by MTV presumably because the word *devil* as used in the song stands for all white people. It could not have been the lyrics that caused the ban because lines like "Then spit on your flag and government/Cause 'help the black' was a concept never meant," although militant, are not nearly as fiery as songs written by other rappers during the conscious movement. Paris followed that up with 1992's *Sleeping With the Enemy*, an album that contained a song called "Bush Killa." The artwork for that tune showed Paris holding an assault rifle while President George H. W. Bush is giving a speech. Distributors were afraid to handle the album, so Paris released it himself. *Sleeping With the Enemy* sold 400,000 copies. His latest album, *Sonic Jihad*, covers the need to stop police brutality and Black-on-Black violence.

Public Enemy

Although rap music was a constant in my household, I had never heard a sound like Public Enemy (or "P.E." as a lot of people called them on the street). The group was formed on the campus of Adelphi University in Long Island in 1982 and was composed of Carlton Ridenhour aka Chuck D, William Jonathan Drayton, Jr. aka Flavor Flav, Richard Griffin aka Professor Griff, and Norman Rogers aka DJ Terminator X.

These guys were on fire.

I thought their music was the "freshest" shit I ever heard and still do.

"Don't Believe the Hype" encouraged people not to be so quick to believe everything we hear and read in the mainstream media. "Night of the Living Baseheads" was a rhyme that equated being a crackhead to life as a zombie—it was a tale of the horrors of the drug set against the unrelenting sound of DJ Terminator X's alarm. "Black Steel in the Hour of Chaos" was a complicated track with layered messages from the criticism of Black involvement in the military to the treatment and conspiracy behind Black men in prison. "911 is a Joke" was scary/humorous commentary by Flavor Flav on the lax-to-nonexistent service given by police and ambulance workers in predominantly Black neighborhoods, "Welcome to the Terrordome" was jam-packed with references to violence inflicted on the Black community as well as the self-destruction that existed within the community.

And then there was "Fight the Power," which became the soundtrack to filmmaker Spike Lee's masterpiece, *Do the Right Thing*. Spike also directed the empowering music video that was filmed in Brooklyn with crowds of boys wearing high-top fade hairstyles and girls sporting bamboo earrings, marching and pumping their fists as they carried posters of Malcolm X and other heroes.

Queen Latifah

Dana Owens aka Queen Latifah started singing in a Baptist church choir when she was just a young a girl. She started in the rap music industry as a beatboxer for a short-lived rap group called Ladies Fresh. After that job ended, she decided to become a solo artist. Her first album, *All Hail the Queen*, was released in 1989. Three more albums, *Nature of a Sista*, *Black Reign*, and *Order in the Court* followed.

Queen Latifah was tall, plus sized, and had a

commanding presence that demanded respect. Her music dealt with social issues and also challenged the patriarchy in the rap music industry.

"Ladies First" blasts the message that Latifah believes women have a place in rap music and that she can hold her own (on the mic) lyrically with anyone.

"U.N.I.T.Y" won a Grammy Award for its hard-hitting anger about the misogyny in our society, domestic violence, and the need for peace.

"Evil That Men Do" points out that people will gladly pop a quarter in a video game but balk at giving a nickel to a homeless person who has his palm outstretched.

Queen Latifah left the rap music business in 1998 for an acting career in TV and film but she left a permanent feminist streak behind.

Sister Souljah

Activist, writer, and rapper Lisa Williamston aka Sister Souljah was born in the Bronx, New York, in 1964. She attended Rutgers University in New Jersey where she majored in American History and African Studies. Members of the famed rap group Public Enemy discovered Souljah and she became a featured vocalist on many of their songs. In 1992 she released her solo album, *360 Degrees of Power*. Both of the videos from that album, "The Final Solution: Slavery's Back in Effect" and "The Hate that Hate Produced," were banned (as too militant) by MTV. After her career as a rapper was over, Souljah wrote a best-selling novel called *The Coldest Winter Ever*. It sold over a million copies and Jada Pinkett-Smith has optioned it for a feature film.

A Tribe Called Quest

Jonathan Davis aka Q-Tip and Malik Taylor aka Phife grew up together in Queens, New York, and formed their rap group in 1988. Their music focused on important issues like date rape and the sheer stupidity of Black folks running around using the "N" word.

Their debut album, *People's Instinctive Travels and the Paths of Rhythm*, did well but it was their second one, *The Low End Theory*, that is considered an important album in the annals of hip-hop. "Jazz" is a praise song for the roots of Black music. "Rap Promoter" deals with the exploitation of rappers in the music industry.

They weren't nationalists or political but their great storytelling gave young people strong, positive messages to live by and struck a perfect balance of hip-hop and bohemian sensibility.

Tupac Shakur

If this were a book on party rap, Tupac (born Leshane Parrish Crooks) would be included to cover the songs he made in the middle of his career. If this were a book on gangsta rap, he'd make the list because of the recordings he made toward the end of his life. Here, we will focus on the conscious songs that were recorded at the beginning of his career in rap music. He was a complex artist who defied categories in his music, his poetry, and on film.

Tupac's socially conscious songs were megahits that endeared him to millions of people who were so touched by the lyrics that they decided to keep on loving him long after he had moved on to harder and more dangerous tunes.

Dear Mama is the song where Tupac, whose mother was addicted to crack, forgives her for the addiction and the misery that it caused him as a teenager, acknowledges how hard it is to raise kids as a Black, single mother on welfare, thanks mothers around the world for all their sacrifices, and ends up thanking the Lord for giving him a mother at all. Who can forget one of the heartrending lyrics— "and even as a crack fiend mama, you always was a Black queen, mama," or the sweet chorus, "don't cha know we love ya? Sweet lady?" Then there was "Keep Ya Head Up," a rhyme that let women on public assistance know that he realized they weren't welfare queens and told them to hold their heads up high and keep the faith that life would get better. Another important message in the song was that women should always leave a man if he doesn't treat them well. "Holler If You Hear Me" is a shout-out to every wrongfully imprisoned Black man and everyone in the ghetto who has been or will be unfairly harassed by a racist cop. There is also "Trapped," which is chock-full of ways that living in the hood and being imprisoned can lead to a feeling of being helpless and the terrible toll it takes on the human psyche.

Tupac's love for Black people is palpable in all of these songs and it was the loss of this man (not the gangsta rapper who came later) that made us cry on September 13, 1996.

X-Clan

Paradise the Architect, Professor X, Brother J the Grand Verbalizer, and DJ Suga Shaft.

They had it all: songs with political content, Afrocentric clothes, Afrocentric artwork in their videos, and strong-looking sistas with natural hairdos in their videos. It just didn't get any more raw dog than X-Clan. I remember the first time I saw the video for "Funkin' Lesson." There sat Professor X and Brother J—two dark-skinned brothers with big ass loop nose rings, ankhs almost as big as they were, dark suits, crowns . . . the whole nine. These guys were serious, unapologetic, and uncompromising and I loved it. I raced out to get the album and played that tape to death.

Their emphasis on Kemet (this is what ancient Egyptians called their country) led to my interest in ancient Egypt. According to X-Clan, everything Egyptian was my cultural, intellectual, and spiritual birthright.

After that I became obsessed with all things Kemet. I learned all the names of the pharaohs and queens of precolonized Egypt, learned to read hiero-glyphs, and visited the Metropolitan Museum of Art frequently to look at MY ANCESTOR'S STUFF. MY STUFF. It was around this time that I noticed the African wing was separate from the Egyptian wing and it made me angry but it also validated the conspiracy theories I was hearing.

X-Clan caused me to go out and buy a book called *Stolen Legacy* but, since I was only thirteen years old, it turned out to be way over my head.

Who can forget the song called "Fire & Earth"? It told us to ditch the Jheri curls, waves, perms and crimps, pay attention to racism and brutality that just won't seem to go away, wear the nationalist colors of red, black, and green, teach an African how to say Black man, and to remember that the media might call the Black man an animal but in Milwaukee there was a white cannibal (mass murderer Jeffrey Dahmer whose victims were mostly Black males).

Since X Clan members would always tote an African walking stick around in their videos, I bought one, too, and named it Changa. Me and Changa went everywhere together for a long, long time. "The Grand Verbalizer" reminded us to respect religion and gave a shout-out to Moses, Malcolm, and Huey. "Raise the Flag" railed against the folly of relying on the school system to teach us Black history and also managed to sneak in a shout-out to Marcus Garvey.

Although they made other albums, *To the East Blackwards* was my hands-down favorite. It was more than just a rap album. It was a baptism.

YZ

Anthony Hall aka YZ had a very short career and has been all but forgotten by most hip-hop historians. His groove was Afrocentric and the point he was trying to make is that the entire American educational system has a Eurocentric foundation. His songs were never designed or destined to cross over. "Crocodile Dundee" takes its cue from the Nation of Islam and retells their story (accompanied by a terrific, thumping bass line) of Yakub, an evil geneticist who created the white man. "When the Road Is Covered with Snow" exhorts the masses to cover themselves in African history as a defense against all the negative images put forth by the media. "The Master Plan" video was super socially conscious. I loved the video with YZ in his nationalist colors, locks, and those golf-ball-sized red, black, and green beads around his neck walking through the hood. That song got a lot of airplay on a radio show in New York called Rap Attack and everyone was jamming to it at school. It was a wonderful message calling us to empower our community.

It is clear that these complex artists who rapped about the desire for political, social, or economic justice were not creating their music in a vacuum. They were influenced by many, many factors.

One organization that had a major impact on many of them was the Five Percenters.

There are persistent elements of Black Nationalist ideology which underlie and inform both rap music and a larger "hip hop" culture. These elements include a desire for cultural pride, economic self-sufficiency, racial solidarity and collective survival.

—Kristal Brent Zook, Author, *Color by Fox: The FOX Network and the Revolution in Black Television*

2

Droppin' Science and Planet Rock

In the late eighties to mid-nineties it was commonplace to hear references in rap songs and on the street to groups like the Nation of Gods and Earths better known as Five Percenters and the Universal Zulu Nation.

In fact, many of the most popular, well-respected, and complex lyricists at the time were members or affiliates of one, if not both, of these organizations. Membership or influence could be noted through the names that artists chose, iconography in videos or on their clothing, and the lyrics of their records.

Although both organizations existed before the golden age of rap, it was the popularity of conscious hip-hop that made "new-schoolers" interested in joining their ranks. Those who didn't join simply mimicked involvement by talking the talk.

It was commonplace in many parks, storefronts, and street corners in the hood to see a group of young men in a circle discussing literature, history, politics, and cosmology. These meetings, called "ciphers," gave "righteous" men the opportunity to bond, but the main objective was to "drop science" or give each other information.

A Five Percent cipher usually begins with the question, "What's today's math?" This is a reference to the system of associating numbers and letters to a concept created by their founder, Clarence 13X, known by Nation members as "The Father."

Clarence 13X Smith was born Clarence Smith in Virginia in 1929 and moved to New York City in 1946. Several years later he joined the Nation of Islam, replaced his "slave name" with "13X," and attended the famous Temple Number 7, which was then under the leadership of Malcolm X. In 1963, Clarence 13X left the Nation of Islam because he disagreed with the concept of Allah as a God in heaven.

He taught instead that the Blackman ("Black" referring to any of the "original" people—Black, Brown, Red, or Yellow) was "God" and needed to stop believing in fiction and control his own destiny. He taught his followers that 85 percent of the world population consisted of the uncivilized mass that is dumb, deaf, and blind to its own exploitation . . . mentally dead and easily led in the wrong direction but hard to be led in the right one. Smith declared that 10 percent of the population consists of those who create the uncivilized mass and don't truly believe in anything but profit. He said that 10 percent of the population teach the ignorant mass lies and propaganda in order to make themselves rich.

Finally, the remaining 5 percent of the population consists of the civilized people who recognize the lost state of the 85 percent, are aware of the trickery of the 10 percent, and live by the "each one teach one" philosophy —meaning they are ready, willing, and able to teach the truth to seekers of knowledge.

According to Clarence 13X, it is the moral duty of the 5 percent to civilize the uncivilized masses.

Those who believe in the doctrine of Clarence 13X are referred to as "Five Percenters" even though their official name is the Nation of Gods and Earths. Members of the Five Percenters refer to male members as "God" out of respect for their inherent divinity and female members as "Earth" in recognition of a woman's power to produce and bear fruit. The "fruit" can be literally interpreted as the ability to birth children or as the fruit of wisdom.

Clarence 13X also urged his students to wake up and realize that Islam was the true path of the righteous. Islam being broken down to I-Self-Lord and Master (I.S.L.A.M) and Allah being broken down to

Arm-leg-leg-Arm-Head aka Hue-man (A.L.L.A.H.), a usage of terms that continues to infuriate traditional Muslims to this day.

In 1967, with the help of New York mayor John Lindsay, the Five Percenters leased a building on 126th Street and 7th Avenue that still functions as their headquarters. It is called the Allah School in Mecca. Various lectures and seminars are held there. Other meetings, known as Parliaments, are held at a nearby school. At the Parliaments, topics of discussion stem from whatever number constitutes the "day's mathematics."

Figuring out the "day's mathematics" takes a basic knowledge of conventional numerology and the specialized knowledge of how that number relates to the teachings included in the Book of Life or lessons from the Nation of Islam. For example, if today is July 23, then add 2 + 3, which equals 5. The number 5 according to "Supreme Math" equals the concept of "Power Refinement." Here is a breakdown of what the Nation calls the "Supreme Mathematics."

1. Knowledge
2. Wisdom

3. Understanding
4. Culture/Freedom
5. Power/Refinement
6. Equality
7. God
8. Build/Destroy
9. Born
10. Cipher

Inside a Parliament

If a person is interested in addressing the audience, it is proper to line up on the side of the stage and wait patiently until someone else has finished speaking. There is no time limit to how long anyone can speak. Some speeches are as short as four minutes, others as long as forty minutes.

When I was invited to attend, I was a bit nervous because I wasn't sure if it was really a peaceful group or not. I shouldn't have been nervous. The atmosphere was extremely relaxed. This was great since I had a lot to say about the topic at hand. Then I noticed that none of the other women were speaking. In fact, most of the women were not even in the auditorium. Most were selling goods in the hallway, caring for children, or preparing food. The women who were in the auditorium acted in a supportive capacity, instead of an active one.

I was disappointed, because I had prepared bulleted notes listing the things I wanted to discuss, but I wasn't sure how I would be received.

I listened to what all the men had to say but internally I was screaming at the other women to get the hell up and say something. It never happened.

After a few more speeches I couldn't take it anymore. When the host asked if anyone else would like to say something, I stepped forward. I will never forget the expressions of shock, disbelief, and outrage in the eyes that followed me, including those from the women in the back.

The host smiled courteously as he stepped aside. He was supportive of what was obviously a bold move, but still a bit uncomfortable. I discussed the deterioration of mainstream hip-hop and its negative effect on the children. Some men loosened up and nodded their heads in agreement. Others still looked like deer caught in the headlights. Two or three men were just plain pissed and walked out. I continued my ten-minute diatribe and humbly accepted the applause that followed.

Externally I was cool but inside I was a pit of boiling lava because it reminded me of a conversation I had had with two members of the Nation back in 1996.

A few of my friends and I were hanging out in Washington Square Park in Greenwich Village. A cipher formed at one of the empty chess benches. We were invited to "add onto the site" and joined them in a discussion on familial duty. I was incensed as soon as a few of the guys began placing the blame for the deterioration of family values solely on women who didn't know their place.

The most outspoken man said that women are represented by the moon and men are represented by the sun. Therefore women are a reflection of the sun's power and shouldn't try and be the power itself.

Having an interest in world mythology, I casually mentioned the fact that in many cultures it was the female that was represented by the sun. He didn't want to hear anything I had to say. A few of the other guys in his group seemed to agree with a lot of the points I made during the cipher, but they didn't speak up and risk being labeled "soft."

I mentioned this memory to the host after the Parliament had ended and he pulled me aside to talk about it. He admitted to the extremely patriarchal values of many of the men and women in the Nation but he assured me that he was different and was truly proud when I got up to speak. He shook his head with disappointment that things were slow to change but he quickly perked up at the idea of me being the "key to enlightenment."

I told him that I might return someday but declined the invitation to be the Five Percenter feminist crusader.

Since then, I have met a few more male Nation members who don't share extremely patriarchal views.

Of course, we live in a patriarchal society but there is something else that compounds their views.

That something else is prison.

It is a fact that many members of the Nation were introduced to the group and its doctrine while serving time in jail. Prison is a hostile, hypermasculine, homoerotic environment devoid of any positively meaningful contact with women.

Like many other groups that form in prison based on a particular ideology, their primary purpose is survival. Men in prison must rely on each other for comfort by forming tightly knit bonds whether they be platonic or sexual. The more often they return to jail, the more likely they will be comfortable in the company of other men or their "homies" and grow emotionally and spiritually alienated from women.

When ex-convicts return to their neighborhoods, they pass on this way of thinking to their friends who have never been to prison. These friends, often unaware of the psychological damage of the individual influencing them, blindly follow the way of being and acting like "real men." The risk of this happening grows even greater if the youth has few or no other examples of Black manhood outside of the media. This is the plight of many young urban males who have either been to prison or who spend a lot of time in the company of those who have. A lot of the prison-based ideas spread to everyone else through the conduit of hip-hop.

As a community, Nation members have been unfairly labeled a "gang" and a security threat by prison officials. They have fought legal battles with the authorities for the right to identify themselves as a Five Percenter without being punished.

Some states even go so far as to segregate Nation members from the rest of the prison population, not because they have caused any trouble but as a preventative measure in case they decide to do so.

Many in the Nation believe it is simply a case of discrimination against their beliefs, because other clearly defined groups are allowed to integrate with the general population. This is obviously a violation of the Five Percenters' constitutional rights and, as a result, some file suit in protest but they are always ruled against in court.

Nation members are also refused the right to possess Five Percent literature in prison.

However, lack of access to the written word will not hinder the teachings from spreading in the Black community. African American culture was, is, and always will be a word-of-mouth culture at its core. It is this ability to spread complex messages to the community in code through dance, music, clothing, hairstyles, and other modes of expression that have allowed Black people to survive.

The Nation of Gods and Earths have their own language that has been shared with everyone through hip-hop.

Artists from the conscious era of rap music like Brand Nubian, Nas, and Eric B. and Rakim frequently make reference to Five Percenter beliefs in their songs.

The Universal Zulu Nation

The Universal Zulu Nation (U.Z.N.) was founded in 1973 by Bronx hip-hop pioneer Afrika Bambaata. The U.Z.N. is named after the South African nation whose warriors valiantly resisted European imperialism in the nineteenth century.

Bambaataa was determined to be a positive force in the community and, after a soul-inspiring journey to Africa, his goal was to spread the message of non-violent resolution to the youth.

Originally, the Zulus mostly functioned as a dance crew but, as time went on, they developed into a movement to preserve hip-hop in its truest artistic form and create self-awareness.

Members of the Zulu Nation come from all racial backgrounds and religions.

It is important to reemphasize that the Zulus are not a political or religious organization but a social one. Zulu members believe it is pointless to try and change the world around you for the better if you are not aware of yourself or other people first. It is because of this that the Universal Zulu Nation Web site includes sections on U.S. history, world history, health, poetry, law, and esoterica.

U.Z.N. has chapters all over the United States and in over twenty countries around the world including Puerto Rico, Brazil, France, Korea, Poland, Japan, and New Zealand. U.Z.N. also has its own clothing line under the name Sedgwick & Cedar, the address in the Bronx where the hip-hop block parties first began back in the seventies.

Few of today's teenagers know that it was Zulu Nation members like the Rock Steady Crew who put out some of hip-hop's first records and established hip-hop's first radio shows like Africa Islam's *Zulu Beats* on independent radio station WHBI.

The U.Z.N. are also responsible for holding national and international conferences to reestablish responsible hip-hop, mentoring children at risk, and fighting for the freedom of political prisoners like Mumia Abu Jamal.

Like the Nation of Gods and Earths, many young men discover the U.Z.N. in prison. In spite of their emphasis on peace and personal responsibility, many members of the press still imply that they are a gang.

Luckily, hip-hop fans who came of age in the 1980s clearly remember the positive peace-loving messages of the Native Tongues, the Jungle Brothers, De La Soul, and A Tribe Called Quest that kept the Universal Zulu Nation in the spotlight during the late eighties and very early nineties.

A community is democratic only when the humblest and weakest person can enjoy the highest civil, economic, and social rights that the biggest and most powerful possess.

—A. Philip Randolph, Civil Rights Activist

3

Wake Up!

The Black image in Hollywood has been a subject of controversy since the early days of the silver screen. During the golden age of American cinema (the '30s and '40s), Black people were mostly characterized as dim-witted but well-intentioned servants, hungry cannibals with a craving for cauldron-stewed white flesh, or dancing darkies.

During the 1950s and 1960s there were variations of the aforementioned roles but then came the gangster films of the 1970s, films that have been labeled "Blaxploitation" movies. In these movies, Black folks battled against "The Man" and won. It is no wonder that they were extremely popular in the Black community. The only problem is that with few exceptions (like *Shaft*, starring Richard Roundtree) the hero was usually a pimp or someone else living on the wrong side of the law. Most of the rappers are too young to have actually seen these films in a movie theater. But they know the plots and lots of the dialogue from stories oft-told by their older relatives and, later, through the new life that these films received on videocassettes that could be purchased or rented. Rap music lyrics and videos are riddled with references to these films.

In the '80s we saw the rise of the Black cop like Eddie Murphy in *48 Hours*, Danny Glover in *Lethal*

Weapon, or the far less popular (but equally talented) Carl Weathers as *Action Jackson*.

More recently, we have been inundated with "Hollyhood" films set in the ghettos of every major city in the country. These films overwhelm the audience by the sheer ugliness of the worlds depicted without explaining how the situations got so bad. They do not address issues like the elimination of arts programs in schools, the closing of neighborhood afterschool school centers, the lack of jobs and opportunity, the draconian drug laws, etc. Without a reasonable explanation for the on-screen thuggery, young Black males appear as the same bloodthirsty savages that Hollywood portrayed on-screen decades ago.

Hollywood also loves to pump out "Great White Hope" movies where a white person comes from the good part of town to help motivate the street kids or, if the movie is set outside of the United States, to dazzle noble savages with their greatness. Whether it is *Rambo*, *Dangerous Minds*, or *The Last Samurai*, the message is always the same: Blacks should thank God that they are not without the inspirational guidance and unrelenting courage of the brave and caring Caucasian.

But in the late eighties and early nineties, there were many films that made the conscious rappers think about specific challenges faced by the Black community in a different way:

Boyz n the Hood—1991

The summer of 1991 saw the birth of the "urban drama"—movies that depicted the plight of young Black males in the war-torn streets of the ghetto. However, Boyz n the Hood should not be lumped in with the ridiculous and oversimplified stories about ghetto thuggery that came later. It is a coming-of-age story. It is a boys-will-thrive-if-they-have-morally-strong-smart-and-dedicated-fathers story. It is a strive-toward-college-even-if-bullets-and-death-surround-you story. It is not a story of gangbanging as sport and there is no bloodshed until the very end of the film.

The main character, Trey, is the ten-year-old son of striving parents, who moves to live with his father in Compton while his mother pursues her career goals. Although he is used to spending summers with his dad and is well known and liked by the kids in the neighborhood, he is clearly different from them with his "proper" speech, factual knowledge, and discipline. We are immediately drawn into and horrified by the harsh world that Trey and his little friends are growing up in, but we are amused and saddened by their childish interpretations of what is going on around them as they try and make sense of their lives.

The film jumps ahead seven years to the adolescence of Trey and his friends. It is here that we become educated about the vicious cycle of hopelessness and violence that these boys have little chance of escaping. As our awareness increases, everyone, including the villains of the movie, become multidimensional and even sympathetic characters.

When Trey is faced with a choice to follow his peers on a revenge-fueled rampage or go back home and not participate in the plan, it is a defining moment, and the message of the film becomes crystal clear: Good parenting and positive Black fathers produce responsible sons.

Trey's dad taught him that thinking consciously and acting responsibly were the keys to real manhood, not toting a gun and acting tough, a lesson that his other friends were never taught. Most importantly, Trey's dad lived as he taught.

It is a rich, engaging tale that posed serious questions.

The conscious rappers got the message and their lyrics frequently contained reminders to fathers that their sons were watching the way they lived.

Daughters of the Dust—1991

Julie Dash brought us the story of the Peazant family. They are "Geechees" or "Gullah" people, descendants of enslaved Africans sent to the South Carolina sea islands to work on indigo plantations. Because they were isolated, they retained many African customs including ancestor reverence, storytelling, and basket weaving. The Peazants are preparing for life on the South Carolina mainland and the story is told from the point of view of an unborn child who belongs to a main character named Trula.

The unborn child explains the complexities of relationships and the even more complex circumstances surrounding her birth.

The Paezant struggle is one between the old and the new. The grandmother refuses to leave the place where her ancestors toiled. Her children want to leave as quickly as possible and become "modern."

There is no right or wrong.

As the movie unfolds, it becomes clear that the family will cease to be a tight-knit unit once they cross the water to mainland civilization.

The young Peazants envision a paradise on the other side. We know there is no paradise and wonder how they will survive, coming from a completely self-sufficient community that makes their own clothes, catches their own food, and builds their own houses.

In addition to the broader theme of defining what is and what isn't "civilized," we are also kept on the edge of our seats wondering if the relationship between the parents of our beloved unborn protagonist is going to work out. It is a beautiful film with gorgeous people and images of the sea island's natural beauty that is both haunting and unforgettable.

The conscious rappers made the point that not many Black people know their own history.

How many people knew about the Gullahs or Geechees before *Daughters of the Dust* was released?

Do the Right Thing—1989

Film critics who screened this film before it was released insisted that it would cause Black folk to riot in the streets and that Spike Lee was wrong to create it and should be responsible for the subsequent civil unrest after it was shown.

It was a ridiculous and insulting position to take. If Black folk rioted every time there was a questionable shooting of a young Black male by a police officer, there would be at least three riots a year whether Spike Lee decided to become a filmmaker or not.

It is the story of events that unfold on a block in Bedford-Stuyvesant, Brooklyn, on one of the hottest days of the year. The stifling heat serves as a metaphor for the rising racial tensions between whites and Blacks in the neighborhood.

The protagonist, Mookie, played by Lee himself, is a delivery boy at a pizzeria and as we follow him throughout his day we get a glimpse of all the colorful characters that he knows so well. We are introduced to Sal, the owner of the local pizzeria; his sons, Pino and Vito; Radio Raheem, a boom-box carrying hip-hopper; Buggin Out, an eccentric, politically-minded young man; and a host of others. Spike Lee makes clear what he thinks of Buggin Out through the name that he gives this character. In the street slang of the time, the term buggin' out meant going crazy.

Although Lee makes us aware of the offensive stereotypes people have of each other with the use of individually wrapped monologues and in-depth conversation with Sal's son Pino that are as serious as they are hilarious, the fuel doesn't hit the fire until Buggin Out asks Sal why there are no pictures of Black people on the wall of the pizzeria.

Sal, a proud Italian American, has pictures of Al Pacino, Sophia Loren, Joe DiMaggio, and other famous Italians on the wall and is initially shocked and then offended by the question.

Buggin Out makes the point that his business is in a Black neighborhood and that all of the people who buy his food are Black.

Sal (who is beloved by everyone in the neighborhood) won't take the pictures off the wall. He tells

Buggin Out to get his own business and do what he wants with the walls.

Buggin Out decides to start a boycott against Sal's Pizzeria. No one listens to him. No one wants to boycott Sal's.

Radio Raheem is another character in the film. A perfect symbol of hip-hop strength and hip-hop rebellion. His radio (which only plays "Fight the Power" by Public Enemy) speaks for him and other young Black people who are living in a time that is rife with racial tension and economic pressures.

One day, Radio Raheem is buying pizza and Sal tells him in a very abrasive way that he cannot have his boom box radio on when he enters the pizzeria. Sal cannot stand rap music. Especially loud rap music.

When Buggin Out runs into Radio Raheem and tells him about the proposed boycott, Raheem is more than happy to join the boycott.

Tensions continue to escalate until Radio Raheem becomes a victim of police brutality and is tragically killed. As a result, the neighborhood erupts in protest and destroys the pizzeria, leaving many innocent people victimized and arrested.

Do the Right Thing was a protest film seen through a hip-hop lens. Most of the characters were under thirty with a hip-hop aesthetic, and the conscious rap group Public Enemy provided the booming, take-no-prisoners, fight-against-the-forces-that-keep-Black-people-down soundtrack.

Get On the Bus—1996

By the time *Get On the Bus* was released, the conscious era had already lost influence in the era of the gangsta rapper.

Otherwise, Black Americans would have packed to see the new Spike Lee joint instead of *Booty Call* that weekend.

However, the film represents the last point in that golden era of rap when intelligence was considered cool.

Spike Lee decided to make a film about the Million Man March, which had been organized by Minister Louis Farrakhan in an attempt to empower Black men to do more in their communities.

The film follows a busload of characters who are on their way to the march in Washington, DC. The characters have very little in common but they are on the bus and, therefore, must interact with each other for a couple of hours.

During the journey Spike uses the characters to ask a number of questions: What is the role of the Black gay male in his community? Should women have been invited to the march, too? Was Farrakhan the proper person to organize such an event? When is it too late to assume responsibility as a man and a father?

Hollywood Shuffle—1987

Robert Townsend maxed out all his credit cards to bring this satire of the Black experience in Hollywood to the screen. Cowritten with Keenen Ivory Wayans, it was a comedic masterpiece with serious social commentary on racial stereotypes.

Bobby Taylor is a young, talented Black actor with dreams of winning an Oscar. He has dreams of playing the first Black superhero or perhaps a detective who solves crimes using his intellect. Bobby daydreams a lot about the leading-man roles he could play. None involve the role of street thug.

When his agent calls for him to audition for the lead role in a film, Bobby and his family are ecstatic.

His dreams are shattered at the audition when the casting directors ask him to coon up in order to win the role of a gang leader named Jimmy. The people in charge don't just want a good portrayal of a gang leader. They pressure him to make Jimmy "more Black." In other words, stick his butt out more, walk in a super-exaggerated pimp roll, and use gestures that only exist in screen portrayals of Black street toughs.

The film shows Bobby struggling with the morality of taking such an offensive role.

There are many laugh-out-loud scenes such as one where Bobby imagines the NAACP protesting angrily in the background as the leader of the NAACP played by Paul Mooney says into a journalist's microphone, "We'll never play the Rambos unless we stop playing the Sambos!"

Hollywood Shuffle is mostly comprised of skits that weave perfectly together with the theme of the movie and we are satisfied at the end when Bobby decides (like the conscious rappers) that the dignity of his people is worth more than dollars and cents.

Jungle Fever—1991

There have been a few films that dealt with the subject of Black-white interracial relationships like 1967's *Guess Who's Coming to Dinner* (in which Sidney Poitier plays a super-educated and successful man who has to prove that he is worthy enough to marry a very ordinary and not particularly beautiful white girl), but nobody delved as deeply into the subject from both a Black and white perspective as Spike Lee in *Jungle Fever*.

Flipper, played by Wesley Snipes, is a talented architect who is married to a beautiful department-store buyer named Drew. They live in a luxurious Harlem brownstone and have a cute little girl named Ming. Their lives are the picture of Black upper-middle-class comfort and all is well until Flipper begins to have an adulterous affair with an Italian American secretary named Angela.

Flipper and Angie have nothing in common except sexual curiosity about each other due to race.

Things hit the fan when their respective families find out about the relationship and we watch how their lives slowly unravel as a result. During the course of the movie we get a chance to view all the characters' perspectives on race and how those perspectives affect everything from local politics to communal relations.

The movie also deals with other issues like the plight of the Black professional in getting proper recognition and compensation on the job as well as the devastating effects on a family when one of its members becomes addicted to drugs.

However, it is through the words of Flipper's elderly father (played by the late Ossie Davis) that the feelings of many conscious rappers (as evidenced by their lyrics) were revealed. The father is enraged that his son has lost his Black wife and child (Flipper's wife refuses to forgive him and wants a divorce) just to experience sex with a white woman, like so many Black men who have come before him.

Malcom X—1992

When Malcolm X died in 1965, Ossie Davis delivered a stirring eulogy in which he called Malcolm "our shining Black prince who didn't hesitate to die because he loved us so."

The Shining Black Prince came to life on the silver screen in a cinematic masterpiece by Spike Lee. Brilliantly acted by Denzel Washington, the film made an impact from the first eight seconds until the last credit rolled up.

It told the story of how a small-time hustler named Malcolm Little who called himself Detroit Red became one of the greatest men in American history.

As a result of the film, a whole Malcolm fashion market sprang up in the Black community with either his face or an "X" logo on everything from T-shirts, jeans, and even sneakers.

Most conscious rappers use Malcolm's image, theories, or actual taped voice as part of their acts.

Sankofa—1993

One of the messages that conscious rappers worked very hard to impress upon the populace was that all Black people have been, still are, and will continue to be in the same boat. That boat is the fight against injustice based on skin color and, the rappers said, no Black person can escape it.

The point is bought home in this film.

Sankofa is the story of a Black fashion model named Mona who is on a modeling shoot on the beaches of Gorée Island in West Africa. As she struts in front of the lens of the photographer's camera, she is oblivious to the sacred ground upon which she walks—the ground where many Africans were held captive before being shipped off to the New World never to be seen again by their friends and family.

As Mona takes a tour through the castle, she is as detached and unresponsive as a group of white tourists in the background. Then she is trapped in one of the rooms and transported back in time to live in the shoes of one of her ancestors.

When Mona goes back in time, she becomes a house slave named Shola who is raped repeatedly by her master but sashays past the dirty, overworked, and often mutilated field slaves as they cut sugar-cane. Shola is a practical woman whose sole mission is to survive, and in that world in order to do that a Black person must have the same fear of the white man as he or she has of God almighty. Shola's only two field friends are a man whom she loves named

Shango (played by reggae artist Mutabaruka) and an African-born woman named Nunu.

We witness and feel Shola's pain as she literally faces one disaster after another in juxtaposition with her expanding self-awareness about what it truly means to be an African.

Sankofa is a film heavily laden in metaphor and is not for the faint of heart. The depictions of American slavery are a far cry from the sanitized scenes in *Roots* and other made-for-TV movies that show healthy, well-fed, well-dressed slaves with not a scratch on them or a hair out of place. It is a film that shows the torture, brutal killings, and rapes of Black women, men, and children by their masters.

Sankofa was seen by the conscious rappers as a message to successful models, actors, and other members of the Black monied class who look down on their brethren in the ghetto: Every Black American is cut from the cloth of slavery and that should never be forgotten.

School Daze—1988

"I'm building me a home" boomed out of the surround-sound speakers as a series of black-and-white photos documented the African American journey from slavery to the present. It was a powerful and moving introduction to a brave and brilliant film that has never received the recognition that it truly deserves.

This is a movie about life on America's predominately Black college campuses. It is a story about color discrimination within the Black community. It is a love story between an idealistic young student and his long-suffering and patient girlfriend. It is a plea to Black folk to start sending money to support historically Black colleges instead of relying on white liberal philanthropists to keep them alive.

Vaughn "Dap" Dunlap, played by Laurence Fishburne, is an Afrocentric student activist who wants Mission College to divest from South Africa because of their racist apartheid system. But he is disappointed when he is threatened with expulsion by school administrators, who are Black men. Dap assumes that they are simply Uncle Toms but they are not. They know that if the rich white people who support Mission College become angry, the whole school would be in danger of shutting down. It was a profound point that didn't provoke as much dialogue as the intraracial prejudice that took place on the campus.

It is truly a testimony to Spike Lee's genius that *School Daze* managed to be funny and entertaining and didn't collapse under its own weight (apartheid, love, hazing, poor Blacks vs. well-off Blacks, light-skinned Blacks vs. dark-skinned Blacks).

The conscious rappers used history lessons (light-skinned Blacks received better treatment than dark-skinned Blacks during slavery) to hold a mirror up to the community and rapped very, very hard for things to change.

I began to get industry pressure to make gangster style rap records and this was, in my opinion, the ultimate hypocrisy. The very industry that was fighting not to play rap records, touting its potential negative influence on society, was now finding ways to play edited versions of violence-laden gangsta rap.

—Kool Moe Dee, *There's A God on the Mic*

4

Sign of the Times

Conscious groups like Public Enemy had a great deal to rap about from 1987 to 1996. During this time period, the community was riveted to some of the most explosive racial incidents in the post–Civil Rights era.

Not all of the events took place in New York but, since the conscious rappers were mostly from various parts of New York City, that is the focus here.

African Americans had a great deal to be angry about during this time and the conscious rappers articulated that anger over a thumping bass beat.

The hip-hop generation can remember a time when blatant injustice was called exactly what it was, without the cooling effect of pop psychologists on talk shows that promoted "loving everybody because we're all human" without addressing the grievances of the oppressed or confronting those in power that prevented the manifestation of this mythologized "love."

On the rare occasions that these pop psychologists deal with uncomfortable issues surrounding race, class, or gender in America, the topic is given short shrift and then the host or another guest quickly brings up our common humanity, not as a tool to move people to action against injustices but as a reset button to get the audience to smile and applaud.

Fans of sociopolitical rap music knew this all too well and that is why Chuck D said that rap music was the "Black CNN" because rappers would constantly make references to national and world events that were hurting Black people.

The conscious rappers provided the only forum where young Black people could express how they felt about the topic of the day. Before conscious rap and now that it is rarely heard, young Black people were absent from any meaningful discourse in relation to contemporary issues. The loss of this tradition in hip-hop is devastating because it makes young people totally oblivious to or nonchalant about what's going on in the world around them even when something may ultimately adversely affect their own community.

Fifteen years ago, it was commonplace to hear youth discussing the subject matter presented to them through the music.

References to many of the following occurrences can be found in the lyrics written by the conscious rappers.

Eleanor Bumpers—1984

Eleanor Bumpers was a sixty-nine-year-old, mentally disturbed Black woman who, because she weighed 275 pounds, lumbered along when she walked. She lived alone in a one-bedroom apartment in the Bronx section of New York City. She paid $96.85 per month in rent—money from her monthly social security check. When the city did not make some requested repairs in her apartment, she stopped paying the rent. Mrs. Bumpers lived in a high crime area and most elderly women in the building did not feel safe. So, when a representative from the Housing Authority showed up to find out why she had not paid the rent, Mrs. Bumpers carried a kitchen knife at her side while she explained what was wrong. Then she closed the door.

A social worker called her on the phone. She said that he was "stupid" and that her rent had been paid.

The social worker called in a psychiatrist.

Mrs. Bumpers answered the door, carrying her kitchen knife. The psychiatrist would later testify that she held the knife "like a security blanket" and that during the interview, he never felt that he was in danger of being attacked. In fact, once Mrs. Bumpers became comfortable with him, she placed the knife down on a nearby windowsill and left it there. During the interview, Mrs. Bumpers said that President Ronald Reagan and Cuban president Fidel Castro had killed her children and that she was being forced out of her apartment because the city wanted to use it as a whorehouse. She clearly needed to be hospitalized and the psychiatrist left the apartment, determined to see that she got the help that she needed.

The city decided that it was best to evict her from the apartment first and then hospitalize her.

The police officers who showed up had been warned that Mrs. Bumpers was a violent, emotionally disturbed person who might be carrying a kitchen knife and could also be armed with hot lye to throw in their faces. It has never been made clear where they got the story of the lye.

In any case, five police officers showed up wearing protective vests and gas masks or goggles.

Did they look like aliens to an old, scared, mentally disturbed person?

She ran at them with the knife.

Officer Stephen Sullivan shouted three warnings to "drop the knife."

She did not.

Officer Sullivan pumped a 12-gauge shotgun and fired. The shot blew off the hand that was holding the knife.

He pumped again and shot her square in the chest.

Eleanor Bumpers died in the emergency room of Lincoln Hospital.

Angry New Yorkers demanded to know why five police officers did not even try to wrestle a knife out of the hand of an elderly overweight woman.

Stephen Sullivan went before a grand jury because, when the second shot was fired, Eleanor Bumpers was not a danger to herself or the officers. She no longer had the knife or a hand to hold it in.

In the end, the powers that be decided it was a case of justifiable homicide and none of the officers was disciplined.

Bernhard Goetz—1984

On the afternoon of December 22, 1984, five males went downstairs into a Manhattan subway station and boarded the #2 express train headed downtown. They were Berhnard Goetz, age thirty-seven, Barry Allen, age nineteen, Troy Canty, age nineteen, James Ramseur, age eighteen, and Darrell Cabey, age nineteen. According to Goetz, he sat down near the four teenagers and Canty asked, "How are you?" After Goetz replied that he was "fine," Canty then said, "Give me five dollars." Goetz said that he pretended not to understand the request so Canty repeated it. Goetz later told police that at that moment he "snapped" and decided to "murder them, to hurt them, to make them suffer as much as possible." He got up and drew a .38 caliber revolver. Goetz shot Canty in the chest, Allen in the back, Cabey in the left side severing his spinal cord and leaving him wheelchair-bound for life, and Ramseur in the arm. Later, in a police statement, Goetz said, "If I had had more bullets, I would have shot them again, and again, and again." The four teenagers all lived, though Darrell Cabey also suffered brain damage in addition to being rendered a paraplegic.

Bernard Goetz was white. The four teenagers were Black.

Goetz got off the train, rented a car, and drove

out of New York State. In Bennington, Vermont, he buried the weapon and the jacket that he had used while committing the crime.

The newspapers immediately took Goetz's side. Several reported as fact that Goetz was approached by four Black teens who were brandishing screwdrivers. This contradicted Goetz's own statement to the police in which he said that he did not see any weapons and that he did not believe the boys were armed at all. Reporters quickly did background checks on all four boys. They had all been arrested before although only Cabey had a felony (armed robbery) on his record.

Goetz had also been mugged twice. Once in the mid-1970s and again in 1981. He was injured in the 1981 incident. Now he was a hero. The New York tabloid press dubbed him the "subway vigilante" for shooting the teens before they had a chance to rob him, injure him, or both. Incredibly, C.O.R.E. (Congress of Racial Equality) offered to raise money for his defense.

The city was divided into two groups. There were those who believed that Goetz should be sent to jail for attempted murder and assault because his life was not in danger at the time he pulled the (unlicensed) gun. Others felt, given New York City's staggering crime rate and that robberies were frequently committed by young Black males, that Goetz should not be prosecuted at all.

The Goetz trial was front-page news for over a year.

In the end, Bernhard Goetz was acquitted of attempted murder and all assault charges. He served eight months in jail for illegal weapons possession.

Bernard Goetz is mentioned in the lyrics of LL Cool J, Wu-Tang Clan, and the Beastie Boys.

The Howard Beach Case—1986

Three Black men were driving through the white neighborhood of Howard Beach in Queens, New York, when their car broke down. A group of whites yelled, "Niggers!" but the men—Cedric Sandiford, thirty, Timothy Grimes, twenty, and Michael Griffith, twenty-three—simply ignored them and went into a local pizza parlor. When they emerged from the eatery, they found a group of white youth with baseball bats waiting for them. They set upon Sandiford, Grimes, and Griffith with the bats as the three men desperately tried to escape. Grimes saw a hole in a fence and slipped through it. Sandiford and Griffith ran.

Three of the white guys—Jon Lester, seventeen, Jason Ladone, sixteen, and Scott Kern, seventeen—chased them down and beat them severely. Sandiford finally pretended to be unconscious. Griffith staggered into the path of an oncoming car and was killed.

Griffith's tragic death enraged Black New Yorkers. Crowds of Black people marched through Howard Beach chanting, "Howard Beach, have you heard this is not Johannesburg?" over and over again.

The trial polarized the city.

In the end, State Supreme Court Justice Thomas Demakos sentenced Ladone to five to fifteen years and Kern got six to eighteen years. He saved the stiffest sentence for Jon Lester whom he said "showed no remorse, no sense of guilt, no shame, no fear." Lester was sentenced to ten to thirty years in prison.

Tawana Brawley—1987

Tawana Brawley, fifteen, had been missing for four days from her home in Wappingers Falls, New York.

On November 28, 1987, she was alive and conscious a few feet from an apartment building that her family had once lived in. Tawana's clothing had been torn and burnt. Her body, which was in a garbage bag, was smeared with feces. She was taken to a hospital where hospital personnel found racial slurs written on her body in charcoal. Police officers who saw her at the hospital say that she had an "extremely spacey" facial expression. She only said one word: "neon."

During a subsequent interview, Ms. Brawley said that she had been raped repeatedly by three white men and that one of them was wearing a police officer's uniform.

The Black community was still reeling from the Goetz shooting, the Bumpers killing, and the Griffith murder.

This was just too much.

African Americans from the poorest rungs of society to famed comedian Bill Cosby (who pledged his financial support to Tawana Brawley) were enraged.

Civil rights activist Reverend Al Sharpton along

with lawyers Alton Maddox and C. Vernon Mason took on the case.

Six men ended up accused of rape, but a grand jury decided that there were inconsistencies in Brawley's story and not enough evidence to charge the men with a crime.

Many in the Black community at the time believed that the outcome would have been different if the teenager in question had been a white female and the accused had been Black.

Spike Lee echoed the community's feelings when he prominently displayed the statement, "Tawana told the truth," in graffiti on a brick wall in the film *Do the Right Thing*.

Tawana Brawley and her family moved to the South in the eighties and she still sticks by her story until this day.

The Central Park Jogger—1989

Trisha Meili was a twenty-eight-year-old investment banker who went jogging in Manhattan's famed Central Park on April 19, 1989. She was beaten, raped, and was near death from a fractured skull, hypothermia, and blood loss when a construction worker found her unconscious body. At first, doctors predicted that she would die within hours or end up on a life support system for the rest of her life.

Miraculously, Ms. Meili recovered from her injuries although she had no memory of the violent assault and could not identify her assailant.

The police accused five young men (five Black and one Latino) of the crime. Four of them confessed, but many people believed that the confessions were coerced. The Reverend Calvin O. Butts of Harlem's Abyssinian Baptist Church said, "The first thing you do in the United States of America when a white woman is raped is round up a bunch of Black youths, and I think that's what happened here."

One prominent New York newspaper routinely referred to the accused—Antron McCray, Yusef Salaam, Raymond Santana, Kevin Richardson, and Kharey Wise—as a "teen wolfpack." Famed real estate developer Donald Trump called for their execution.

"The confessions" were videotaped after the boys had been questioned without sleep for at least two days. Their words were chilling: Kevin Richardson said, "Antron got on top, took her panties off." Santana said, "I was grabbin' the lady's tits." Kharey Wise said, "This is my first rape."

The confessions were very important because no blood or DNA tests tied any of the boys, who ranged in age from fourteen to nineteen, to the crime.

They were convicted and served sentences ranging from five to thirteen years.

Black New Yorkers were again furious and compared the case to the infamous Scottsboro case of the 1930s, which ruined the lives of five innocent Black teenagers who were accused of raping a white woman.

In 2002, the rest of the world was stunned to find out that Black New Yorkers had been right all along. Although Antron McCray, Yusef Salaam, Raymond Santana, Kevin Richardson, and Kharey Wise had confessed to beating and raping the Central Park jogger, it was a crime that they did not commit.

In fact, a serial rapist was terrorizing the city during the summer of 1989. He usually tried to stab out the eyes of his victims to prevent identification. He was caught after a string of assaults, including the rape and murder of Lourdes Gonzalez, a woman who died a horrible death right in front of her children. His name was Matias Reyes and he was only seventeen years old at the time. After more than a dozen years in the penitentiary, Reyes started telling people that he was the person who had raped and beaten the Central Park jogger so long ago and that he did it alone.

An investigation was held and, most importantly, Reyes's DNA was tested against the forensic evidence found on the jogger's body.

It was a perfect match.

Yusef Hawkins—1989

Yusef Hawkins was a sixteen-year-old boy who wanted a car but could not afford to buy a brand-new one. There was an ad in a New York paper that a used car was for sale. The price sounded right so he rounded up three of his friends and went to look at it. Unfortunately, the car and its owner were in Bensonhurst, a predominately Italian American neighborhood that wasn't friendly to outsiders. Particularly outsiders with Black skin. It is unclear whether young Yusef was aware of that fact or not. Like most young people, he probably didn't even think of his own mortality.

When the four boys reached their destination, they were approached by a street gang.

The mob chased and beat them.

One of the Italian American boys was armed with a handgun.

He shot and killed Yusef Hawkins.

The Italian American boys said that the killing was not racially motivated. They claimed to have been threatened by an African American gang the week before and that Yusef resembled one of the boys.

African Americans, led by Reverend Al Sharpton, marched in protest through the streets of Bensonhurst.

Many Italian Americans who lived in Bensonhurst were appaled by the killing and called for the perpetrators to be jailed for their crime.

Others shouted racial slurs and spat at the peaceful demonstrators as the television cameras rolled.

Once again, trials were held as African Americans smoldered.

Jospeh Fama, nineteen, the boy who fired the shots, received a sentence of thirty-two years four months in prison. Keith Mondello, also nineteen, received a sentence of five years four months to sixteen years in prison for chasing and beating Hawkins.

Rodney King—1991

On March 3, 1991, a Black motorist named Rodney King was beaten in an extreme case of police brutality by members of the Los Angeles Police Department after a routine traffic stop. King suffered broken bones and teeth, eleven skull injuries, and kidney and brain damage.

There was public outcry as a result of the cold-blooded beating.

For decades, African Americans had been harassed, exploited, and terrorized by the police, but complaints about the mistreatment usually fell on deaf ears. Many in the Black community believed that since the assault was videotaped it would bring national awareness to the hazards of DWB (Driving While Black) and the general mistreatment of Blacks by racist cops, and would subsequently put an end to it.

The policemen went on trial. The verdict stunned Blacks and whites around the world.

On April 29, 1992, the cops were acquitted despite the videotaped evidence. As a result of the unfair verdict, three days of rioting ensued in L.A. that ended in almost a billion dollars in property damage, eight thousand arrests, two thousand injuries, and over fifty people killed.

Jeffrey Dahmer—1991

Jeffrey Dahmer was a monster who preyed mostly on young, gay Black men. Dahmer was a white man. He was also a serial killer, child molester, exhibitionist, necrophiliac, and cannibal. Police in Milwaukee were stunned to find that Dahmer stored human remains in large vats of acid that lined his apartment. Severed heads were found in his refrigerator. No groceries (except for condiments like ketchup and mustard) were found in the kitchen. Dahmer admitted that he frequently ate large portions of his victims. It is because of this that X-Clan lyricist Brother J rapped (in a song called "Fire and Earth") "I remember all the times that you called me an animal but in Milwaukee there's a cannibal." When using the word "me," Brother J is referring to all Black men.

During the Dahmer investigation, the public learned that one of Dahmer's victims, a fourteen-year-old Asian teenager named Konerak Sinthasomphone, managed to escape into the night despite bleeding profusely from the anus and a hole drilled into the back of his head. The blond and Aryan-looking Dahmer ran after him and was struggling to hold him when police appeared on the scene. They believed Dahmer when he said that the drugged boy was his lover and they had just had a lover's quarrel. The police left Konerak Sinthasomphone in Dahmer's apartment. Later, Sinthasomphone's body was dismembered and his skull placed among the others in Dahmer's macabre collection. The other dead men in that collection were all Black males. They included: Curtis Straughter, James Doxtator, Raymond Smith, Ernest Miller, Errol Lindsey, Oliver Lacy, Matt Turner, Anthony Sears, David Thomas, Tony Hughes, and Eddie Smith.

It was hard for anyone to believe that a young, bleeding, and drugged blond white boy would have been left in that apartment with an older Black man. At the very least, they would both have been hauled into the nearest police station until the matter was sorted out.

The police officers were fired.

Dahmer went on trial for fifteen murders in July 1992. He was found guilty and sane. A judge sentenced him to 943 years in prison at the Columbia Correctional Institute in Portage, Wisconsin. On November 28, 1994, a Black inmate named Christopher Scarver beat Dahmer to death with an iron bar.

The police officers who had been fired because of the Sinthasomphone incident were rehired with back pay and praised for their dedication to police work.

The Crown Heights Riots—1991

Gavin Cato and his cousin Angela were outside playing on a Brooklyn street when a car veered up on the sidewalk and struck them both. Both children were Black. Both were only seven years old. Yosef Lifsh, the driver of the car, was white.

Witness accounts differ as to whether Mr. Lifsh

was speeding or not. Everyone, Black and white, agreed that Mr. Lifsh did not deliberately drive the car up on the sidewalk in order to hurt the children.

It was an accident.

Shortly after the accident, an ambulance from the Hatzoloh Ambulance Corps arrived and a police officer allowed the private vehicle to take Mr. Lifsh away for medical attention, even though he was not visibly injured. The mangled children were left on the sidewalk until a city ambulance arrived to take them to the hospital.

Angela would survive her injuries but Gavin would not be so lucky. He died at a nearby hospital.

Black teenagers revolted in response to the cruel and inhuman treatment of the Cato children.

For three consecutive days, the teens rioted, looted, and set fires. Rocks were thrown between large crowds of whites and Blacks.

During the melee, Yankel Rosenbaum, an Australian student who was visiting America, was stabbed to death. He identified an African American teenager, sixteen-year-old Lemrick Nelson Jr., as the person who had stabbed him.

Nelson was acquitted of murder by a state court.

After angry protests, he was then brought up on federal charges of violating Rosenbaum's civil rights. He was sentenced to nineteen and a half years in prison.

And what of the driver, Yosef Lifsh? He did not have a driver's license. He fled the United States and returned to his native Israel to avoid being charged with Gavin's death.

The Simpson and Goldman Murders—
1994–1995

On the night of June 12, 1994, someone stabbed Nicole Brown Simpson and her friend Ron Goldman to death. They were white. Whoever murdered them needed to be taken off the streets and locked away in a penitentiary. Race should not have been an issue.

It was.

The man accused of murdering the two people was Orenthal James Simpson who was rich, Black, and famous. Nicole was his ex-wife.

O.J. Simpson was ordered to turn himself in to the Los Angeles Police Department. Instead, he went on the lam with his best friend, Al Cowlings, at the wheel of the white Bronco. There was no chase. The police simply followed the two men down Interstate 405. Crowds of people (white and Black) lined the interstate, cheering him on. The resulting spectacle with helicopters from news agencies around the country following the former football star was repeated over and over again on almost every television channel. At that time, most white people probably believed that he was innocent of the crimes.

Simpson was taken off to jail. Because of his celebrity, the editors of *Time* magazine decided to publish his mug shot on the cover. O.J. Simpson is a light-skinned African American male. The magazine's illustrator, Matt Mahurin, decided to darken his skin for the cover. He said that he did it to create a more "artful and compelling" picture but Black people felt that it was a deliberate method of playing to the stereotypical "big Black brute" that had appeared again and again in American films and literature.

That was the first volley.

When it was first suggested that Nicole Simpson had been a victim of domestic violence, it was her sister Denise who cried foul to the *New York Post*.

Nicole was a strong woman, she declared, and there was no way she would have put up with being physically attacked by anyone.

Later, it was Denise Brown who would take the stand and offer examples of Simpson's brutality toward his wife.

Simpson's trial began on January 24, 1995, and lasted until October of that same year. It was an exhausting ten months for Blacks and whites alike due to the ugly racism displayed in the courtroom and on the street.

On October 3, 1995, Simpson was acquitted on all charges.

Black people celebrated because the white policemen, who appeared to have been guilty of misconduct during the collection of evidence, did not get away with it. There was also a great deal of pride in O.J.'s lead attorney, a Black man named Johnnie Cochran. The Simpson trial was beamed via satellite to homes around the world. For the first time in history, a Black man (Cochran) was on the world stage, but he wasn't singing, dancing, pleading, or protesting. He had used his brains and American law books to outwit a team of prosecutors.

Whites watched the celebrations and were furious.

Dominick Dunne, a celebrity journalist for *Vanity Fair*, later reported that a rich white couple had fired their happy Black maid on the spot. A white *USA Today* columnist warned that "white women don't riot but they do vote. They can take away your safety net."

It was a threat. A direct threat.

And there were more as white journalists vented their frustration.

Stories spread in the Black community—angry supervisors watched the Black workers for any sign of glee. White/Black friendships unraveled when the Black friend refused to agree that Simpson got away with murder or that Johnnie Cochran "played the race card."

During the days immediately following the verdict, if you were a Black person you could feel the menace in the air. For the first time, young Black people experienced the odd combination of anger and powerlessness in the face of white wrath . . . a sensation that their grandparents had lived with almost daily.

The first recorded rap song was "Rapper's Delight" by the Sugarhill Gang. The lyrics to that song make reference to O.J. Simpson (who was viewed by teenagers of the time as handsome, suave, and well dressed) when the teenagers dream of riding off in a "def OJ," which was slang for a Lincoln Continental automobile.

The Bell Curve—1994

The Bell Curve by Richard J. Hernstein and Charles Murray was published on October 1, 1994.

The authors sought to measure what they considered a large gap in intelligence between the races. The authors hoped that their findings would possibly be used to assist in creating public policies. The 845-page book was heavily publicized and supported by the mainstream media, and much of its content was agreed upon by the American Psychological Association. However, there were many negative critics of it as well for three major reasons: one, because they found the study to be filled with over simplistic data, two, it promoted scientific racism, and three, Murray had no background in psychometrics.

The book disgusted and insulted Black people, who have been the victims of such racist studies in one form or another for hundreds of years.

The fact that the book and its premise weren't immediately disregarded by the masses proves that the same "dumb except for sports and entertainment" mentality about Black people is still alive and well.

In fact, according to an excerpt of the author's initial book proposal, which was printed in the *New York Times Magazine* dated October 9, 1994, the target market for *The Bell Curve* was the "huge number of well-meaning whites who fear that they are closet racists, and this book tells them they are not. It's going to make them feel better about things they already think but do not know how to say."

Apparently there were enough of these "well-meaning whites" to keep it on the best-seller list for weeks and it still sells briskly for the publisher today.

Susan Smith—1994

On October 25, 1994, the country was still split along racial lines over the O.J. Simpson verdict.

Down in Union City, South Carolina, a young white woman put her two young boys (Michael, age three, and Alexander, age fourteen months) in the backseat of a car and pushed the car into a lake to drown them. She told the police that a Black man hijacked her car and drove away with her children in the backseat.

She even gave them a description. That piece of artwork was copied and circulated nationwide.

The teary-eyed mother who begged for the safe return of her two adorable little boys evoked national and international sympathy for what seemed like every parent's worst nightmare.

Nine days later, she admitted to drowning them.

The excuse for murdering her own children was a wealthy lover who rejected the idea of a ready-made family.

However, Blacks were suspicious of her allegations from the beginning. It sounded like the Charles Stuart (a Boston man who shot his wife to death and said that a Black man had done the deed during a robbery gone bad) case all over again.

For the past decade, rap artists—who as informal ethnographers of Black youth culture translate the inarticulate suffering of poor Black masses into articulate anger—have warned of the genocidal consequences of ghetto life for poor Blacks. Their narratives . . . communicate the absurdity and desperation, the chronic hopelessness, that festers inside the post industrial urban center.

—Professor Michael Eric Dyson

5

Kente and Cowries

Like every other culture, hip-hop has its own distinctive fashion. The clothes worn by hip-hop heads during its golden age reflected the need to feel connected to a more welcoming land, to feel powerful even though the Black community appeared to be under siege from outside forces, or to look prosperous even though Reaganomics was grinding its heel into the neck of the poor and the vulnerable.

Back in the day, it was the triple-fat goose coats, thick gold chains, leather bombers, Osh Kosh, Guess anything, aviator jackets, bamboo earrings, wallabees, fifty-four elevens, Ocean Pacific, polka-dots, Bally shoes, Troop, and four finger rings.

The funny thing is how quickly the styles in hip-hop used to change, and it was amazing how every few months an outfit that you cherished just a few weeks prior was suddenly considered "wack."

The dances, slang, and postures would change, too, and if you didn't change just as fast, your friends would burst into laughter at the wrong move, word, or gesture.

Today is nothing like it used to be. A person who died in the latter part of the nineties could crawl out of the grave and ride the subway without anyone blinking an eye because generally the look is still the same. This would not be the case with someone who passed away during the eighties because people would definitely do a triple take at a brother with a gumby, a polka-dot shirt, and Dwayne Wayne glasses or a sister with a mushroom with a super big bang, a miniskirt with spandex underneath, socks, and patent leather shoes.

The conscious era had its own trends, too:

Clock Necklaces

Flavor Flav of Public Enemy popularized the trend of wearing "stopwatch" clock necklaces as a symbol of political awareness by "knowing what time it is." Although Flavor was the comic relief to balance Chuck D's serious demeanor, the stopwatch was a constant reminder to take Flav seriously despite how ridiculous he looked.

Unfortunately Flav is giving his clocks these days to contestants on his ridiculous reality show, *Flavor of Love*, thus sexualizing and neutralizing the original meaning.

Africa Medallions

In the late eighties a well-dressed urban youth wouldn't be caught dead without his or her Africa medallion. The leather necklace had a cutout of the African continent in the disc's center and it was the ultimate symbol of cultural pride.

In the hip-hop classic *Buddy*, Afrika Baby Bam of the Jungle Brothers echoed the sentiment of the time when he said, "Black medallions, no gold," as the ultimate cool accessory. Rappers like Just-Ice popularized wearing a bunch of medallions at the same time.

Red, Black, and Green Necklaces

Necklaces with golf-ball-sized beads in red, black, and green were in fashion for young men around 1990 to 1992. The beads represented the colors of the Black liberation flag, red for the blood of African people shed in the struggle against racism/colonialism, black representing people of African descent around the world, and green representing Africa's lushness and abundance. The flag was created by Marcus Garvey in response to a racist song that was popular in the United States and Britain entitled "Every Race Has a Flag But the Coon" by Will A. Heelan and celebrated patriotic composer J. Fred Helf.

Kente Cloth

Kente cloth is the most well-recognized African textile in America, originating from the Asante and Ewe peoples of Ghana and Togo. The fabric comes in many variations depending on the message the wearer wants to communicate, as many Kente cloths have meanings and/or proverbs that accompany them.

As a result of the renewed interest in Africa during the conscious era, African Americans learned that Kente cloths were traditionally worn by royalty and began wearing it, too, as an affirmation and extension of their own West African heritage. The demand for Kente was so intense that it was appropriated as a surface design for a variety of products including umbrellas, Band-Aids, bookmarks, and balloons. Some Black churches even wore strips of Kente cloth as an Afrocentric choir robe accent.

Cowrie Shell Accessories

Cowrie shells were a symbol of femininity in ancient Egypt and used as currency in precolonial West Africa. The beautiful porcelain-like surface of the marine snail was worn as jewelry, as hair ornamentation, and used to decorate all kinds of objects from sacred masks to dinnerware. Cowrie shell earrings, belts, ankle bracelets, and necklaces were all the rage in the '90s but the trend fizzled and gave way to more Native American–inspired accessories around 1994 like the choker worn by Janet Jackson in her "That's the Way Love Goes" video.

Cross Colours and Karl Kani Urban Wear

Cross Colours was one of the first urban clothing lines and was named Company of the Year by *Black Enterprise* magazine in 1993. That year the Los Angeles–based operation grossed approximately $89 million.

Cross Colours was the uniform for the well-dressed young man around 1992 and nothing got a girl's attention more than one of their denim ensembles with Timberland boots and a Jansport bookbag. Cross Colours was popular before the obsession with darker hues that came with New York's gangsta rap aesthetic. Their jeans came in a variety of bright, fun colors including fuschia, electric blue, orange, and green. The company folded in 1993 because its parent company, Threads 4 Life, could not keep up with the demand for Cross Colours merchandise and its brother company, Karl Kani, at the same time.

However, the end for Cross Colours was just the beginning for Brooklyn-born Carl Williams, who uses the pseudonym Karl Kani ("Can-I") as an affirmation of his capability to succeed. The self-made millionaire, who was not even thirty at the time, not only managed to keep his company afloat during financial hardship, he expanded his product to include designs for women and children and earned huge profits. He also gave back to his community by working with various children's charities and developing an entrepreneurial program at twenty-four elementary schools to teach kids how to run their own business through marketing.

Army Patterned Clothes

The appropriation of Woodland camouflage and other U.S. Battle Dress Uniform (BDU) patterns can be seen heavily around this time period but it is unclear what actually made it popular among dissenters of the establishment. On sight it seems ironic if not plain silly since the military of any nation is trained to shed the blood of those in opposition, but when I asked a Rasta donning a long fatigue printed skirt why she wears it she answered, "I guess I wear it because I represent another kinda army." Subsequent questions yielded similar answers to showing "militancy," but overall, BDU is liked for its comfort, affordability, and durability.

Hemp Products

The nineties was the decade that made the average American aware of potentially dangerous issues affecting the environment, genetically engineered food, and other sci-fi types of horrors. It became trendy for many people to live more "naturally" and exclude pork and beef from their diets, as they were seen to impose increased risk to physical and mental wellness.

However, the trend didn't stop with food. Many conscious young people were wearing clothes and using products made of natural fibers. For a brief period of time a hemp necklace, bracelet, dress, or sandals was the symbol of the "tree-hugger" type as the fad hit primarily among young women.

Hemp was seen as an earth-saving material because it is naturally resistant to UV rays, it preserves nutrients in the soil, and can be grown without the use of harmful, cancer-causing pesticides and herbicides.

Headwraps, Wrap Skirts, and Dashikis

It only made sense that with all the references to Africa in culture that the clothes would follow. Females would buy a few yards of fabric and simply wrap it around their bodies and use the rest of it to cover their heads as high as possible in a tight cylinder-style shape.

Queen Latifah popularized the headwrap.

Erykah Badu added more material for a more dramatic effect in the mid-nineties. Dashikis (worn by both genders) with elaborate embroidery were prized possessions.

Education is the passport to the future, for tomorrow belongs to those who prepare for it today.

—Malcolm X

6

The Sacred Scrolls

One of the greatest things that came out of the conscious era besides the music itself was the emphasis on education and self-improvement.

In a lot of the songs of the day our youth were encouraged to learn about themselves, their history, and how they could effect change in their community and the world around them if they strived toward excellence.

It was a time when people dreamed of getting out of the ghettos rather than glorifying them, the selling and use of illicit drugs was discouraged, Black women were referred to as Nubian Sistas instead of bitches, and lyrics reflected the literacy of the artist who penned them.

It was a time when MCs weren't afraid to show off what they knew for fear of alienating their fans who were just as eager to analyze a complex rhyme line for line and praise the creativity behind it. As a result of their influence many fans rose to the challenge and sought out higher knowledge that consequently brought about the rediscovery of classic Afrocentric literature from the turn of the century and Civil Rights and Black Power Movement eras.

In addition, the genre of street literature in the form of Iceberg Slim and Donald Goines was reintroduced but they were taken for the entertaining cautionary tales they were intended to be and not instructional manuals on how to repeat the mistakes of the doomed protagonists.

Today, what is known as "hip-hop fiction" is in vogue, with all the excitement and drama of the street authors of yesteryear, but many books lack a cohesive story and many writers make up for their lack of structure by inundating readers with graphic, triple-x-rated sex scenes and over-the-top violence. This is, of course, very appealing to young people who view these novels as an extension of the music and that would be fine if they were also reading other things, too.

Part of the reason that eighties kids were more receptive to the nationalistic flavor of music and literature was the sheer fact that many of our own parents had lived through these historic periods in the struggle for liberation and had participated in marches and the like. Many kids now are further removed from this and identify more with ideologies based on lifestyle than color or politics. Adding to this is the superficial appearance of social acceptance because of the infiltration of "Blackness" in popular culture and the resulting attitude that racism, except for rare incidents, happened "back in the day." They seem to think that just because other ethnic groups have adopted the hip-hop aesthetic that it somehow makes everything "all good" without realizing that the same social and economic inequalities of the past still exist, with Blacks still at the bottom of the food chain.

The hip-hop generation today suffers as a result of inadequate public education and a cavalier attitude toward anything nontabloid.

Conscious hip-hop put many on the path to empowerment and these are the books that were the "must reads" during that era:

The Isis Papers
by Dr. Frances Cress Welsing

According to Dr. Welsing, if the nonwhite victims of white supremacy remain unaware of how racism works at its deepest levels and what they must do in order to counteract it, then they will never be able to neutralize the problem.

In addition to the discussion of race, she also

tackles gender and sexuality issues. One of her more controversial and hotly debated comments was that the increasing popularity of Black homosexuality is simply an external behavioral manifestation of over twenty generations of submission to "the man." Welsing also took the time to analyze and decode the sexual symbolism behind everything from Black lingerie, sports involving balls, and phallic-shaped weapons.

The book was ambitious in its range of topics. For example, it also gives tips to Whites on how to aid their healing process by seeking counseling for their race-based anxieties.

Behold a Pale Horse
by William Cooper

Cooper, a former U.S. Naval Intelligence Briefing Team member, penned a cult classic for conspiracy buffs. He claims to reveal jaw-dropping information kept secret by the United States government and gives the reader "insight" into the true intentions of its leaders. From plans to suspend the U.S. Constitution to create a police state to the reasons the AIDS virus was created, it is an intriguing read that seems to eerily coincide with present-day events at some points. Although it can seem a bit over-the-top at times, especially on the subject of extraterrestrials, it is hard to put down.

Iceman Inheritance
by Michael Bradley

Michael Bradley, a white anthropologist, attempts to retrace the prehistoric roots of Caucasoid aggression in an effort to save the world by alerting his people to their racial psychology, a psychology that he claims has brought the world to the brink of disaster. Basically, Bradley claims the origin of the white man's rage is due to the harsh conditions he was forced to endure during the last ice age. He discusses the side effects of glacial adaptation on the Caucasoid mind citing one major defect as the reason for most of the ills of the Western world, the absence of a dualism concept.

According to Bradley, the white man is incapable of accepting paradoxes and interprets them as conflicts instead. This, he says, is a result of the white's own psychology of separation because he himself was alienated from the rest of humanity in the freezing firelit caves of Europe—thus, his innate tendencies to separate instead of synthesizing information first like people of other races.

Bradley also delves deep into the sexist, fear-based erotic history of Europe and compares it to how other cultures have dealt with sexuality and womanhood.

The Willie Lynch Letter and the Making of a Slave

by William Lynch

The Willie Lynch Letter and the Making of a Slave is supposedly a copy of a speech delivered by a British slave owner named Willie Lynch on the banks of the James River in the colony of Virginia in 1712.

Apparently Lynch was invited to America from the West Indies to teach his techniques for brainwashing enslaved Africans to slave owners in the colony.

In the speech he gives detailed instructions on how to create divisions and feelings of mistrust among the enslaved in order to ensure the master/slave relationship for generations.

Historians have since determined that the letter

is a phony and could not have been written during the slave era.

However, it still illustrates in an eloquent and effective way the very real psychological issues that Africans in the diaspora have as a result of centuries of bondage.

Stolen Legacy

by Prof. George G.M. James

In 1954, James outraged the white academic community by stating that what we know as Greek philosophy is actually stolen Egyptian philosophy. In his book he reminds us of the fact that Greek scholars were often educated in Alexandria and that contemporary personalities of their day like Homer described the ancient Egyptians as Black. He compares the similarities between Greek philosophy and the Egyptian mystery schools and cites various ancient sources to support his findings.

James said that he wrote the book to clarify what he felt was a deliberate falsification of history and he attempted to ease race relations by removing the myth of white superiority.

More than fifty years after its publication, James's work is still controversial in academic circles.

Nile Valley Contributions to Civilization and From the Browder File: 22 Essays on the African American Experience

by Anthony T. Browder

Anthony Browder's books were very popular in the nineties and served as an introduction to the ancient Egyptian origin of civilization by giving the reader mind-blowing information on how Africans in Egypt were the originators of astrology, sciences, mathematics, geometry, medicine, and masonry, in one easy-to-read volume.

Browder also explored the negative effects of television on the minds of African American children.

Destruction of Black Civilization: Great Issues of a Race from 4500 B.C. to 2000 A.D.

by Dr. Chancellor Williams

A chronicle of the rise and fall of Black power in the ancient world. The son of an enslaved father,

Williams, found it critical that the next generation have a solid understanding that their history not only precedes the arrival of Arabs and Europeans, but goes back thousands of years before in a flourishing and technologically advanced Egypt.

Civilization or Barbarism: An Authentic Anthropology
by Cheikh Anta Diop

This is another book that uses the lens of anthropology to prove that ancient Egypt was a Black African culture. It analyzes and compares the social structure, physiology, paleontology, archeological, linguistic, and intellectual history with other African cultures. Diop also conducted microscopic analysis on ancient Egyptian mummies using a technique he created called the melanin dosage test to determine their melanin content.

This technique was so groundbreaking that it was later used by the U.S. Forensic Department to determine the race of badly burned accident victims. Diop was determined to help Africa reclaim her history and achievements from those who had stolen it and claimed it for themselves.

Assata: An Autobiography

by Assata Shakur, Angela Davis, and Lennox S. Hinds

Angela Davis and Lennox Hinds put together this memoir of former Black Panther and Black Liberation Army activist Assata Shakur.

Assata was a college student who decided to dedicate her life to the social progress of Blacks in the United States and joined militant organizations to achieve her aim.

In 1973, Assata and two other Black Panthers were stopped in New Jersey for a broken taillight. A gunfight ensued resulting in the death of one of her friends and a New Jersey State Trooper. Despite forensic testing that proved she could not have fired the gun that killed the officer, Assata was convicted of the murders of both her comrade and the state trooper.

In 1979, she escaped from prison. She fled to Cuba in 1984 where she has lived as a fugitive ever since.

From Niggas to Gods

by Akil

Author Akil wrote *From Niggas to Gods* as a self-help manual for young Black inner city males to promote self-awareness, esteem, and respect for self and community. It is clear through this compilation of essays that the author was very much in tune with the complex problems young men growing up in the ghetto face.

His stated goal was to shed light on the "N" word and encourage self-analysis among young people.

Sex and Race: Negro-Caucasian Mixing in All Ages and All Lands: The Old World

by J. A. Rogers

J. A. Rogers put together two volumes on sex and race to destroy the myth of Aryan racial purity by revealing the truth of miscegenation in the bloodlines of even the most "blue-blooded" families of Europe and the Americas. Beautifully illustrated and backed by an impeccable bibliography, Rogers brought the history of human interaction to life.

The book forced readers to question their own views of race.

The Art of War

by Sun-Tzu

This book is the oldest military treatise in the world by an ancient Chinese general and military strategist.

It places an emphasis on understanding the enemy's psychology in order to ensure victory and has been credited with influencing war from Napoleon's battles to Operation Desert Storm.

They Came Before Columbus: The African Presence in Ancient America

by Dr. Ivan Van Sertima

Dr. Van Sertima created a firestorm of controversy with his claims that Africans had visited the Americas centuries before Columbus's historic voyage in 1492. He cited parallels between the Aztec and ancient Egyptian calendars, the existence of crops not native to the Americas, the "Negroid"-looking stone heads of the Olmecs, linguistic similarities between several Native American and West African languages, as well as eyewitness accounts by the Native Americans themselves who told the Spanish of their trades with Black men with spears. In addition, there are the writings of a Spanish priest named Fray Gregoria Garcia, who reported seeing Black people in an Indian settlement.

The Mis-Education of the Negro
by Dr. Carter G. Woodson

Woodson wrote this book in the thirties with the intention of teaching Black people that they had a unique and distinct history in America. This angered many Black middle-class intellectuals of the day who argued that "Negros" were simply Americans. They did not support his effort to get Black studies accepted into school curricula. *The Mis-Education of the Negro* also examines what is now known as "post-traumatic slave syndrome" and asks critical questions about the educational system.

References to all of these books can be found in the lyrics of the conscious rappers.

Rap music is a conversation among and between black youth from one part of the country to another: "What is it like in Detroit, as opposed to L.A., as opposed to New York?"

—Toni Morrison

7

The Black Literati

The eighties was also the beginning of a time when African American women started getting published by mainstream, commercial publishing houses in large numbers and in a variety of genres.

It was not unusual to find middle-class Black females out on shopping sprees for conscious rap tunes and the latest books. Since crack was decimating the Black community and Ronald Reagan's policies left very little money in the inner city, those who were out of work could be found in the public libraries searching for titles.

These authors talked about Black love, self-naming, family, poverty, and how to keep on moving and striving to get through it all.

Baby of the Family
by Tina McElroy Ansa

A coming-of-age novel about a young Black girl growing up midcentury in a middle-class family where appearances are very important.

Beloved
by Toni Morrison

This is a novel in which a woman makes the heartrending decision to murder her daughter rather than let her grow up as a slave.

Disappearing Acts
by Terry McMillan

A love story is set into motion when Franklin, a chronically unemployed construction worker, falls for Zora, a middle-class teacher. This book provides an absorbing view of the racism that pervades the construction industry.

The First Fig Tree
by Vivian Glover

This is a novel set right after World War II in which a girl of seven gets to know her great-grandmother. As the elderly woman tells the story of plantation life and the horrors of slavery, the little girl sees some parallels in her own strictly segregated society where racial violence is common.

Linden Hills
by Gloria Naylor

This is a novel set in the world of wealthy African Americans who have made the decision to mimic the mores of their white counterparts and fall into a world of make-believe in which they decide that their money makes them better than their less-prosperous brethren.

Mama
by Terry McMillan

In this novel the main character is a woman struggling to raise five children on very little money and in a town where there is next to no opportunity for them to grow. This is a very real and balanced look at people who are willing to work but just can't get a break.

1959: A Novel
by Thulani Davis

This book is about the year that Willie Tarrant, a Black girl, turns twelve in Virginia. Through her eyes, the reader experiences the turmoil of the beginning Civil Rights Movement and the meaning of everyday heroism while living with day-to-day terror.

Sisters and Lovers
by Connie Briscoe

In this novel three Black women try to gain self-respect as they cope with day-to-day problems at work and in their families.

Sweet Summer: Growing up with and without My Dad
by Bebe Moore Campbell

The stereotype of the trifling Black father who runs away from his children is brought to a full stop in this poignant memoir about Bebe's youth. Her parents were divorced and she spent every summer with her loving father at his southern home.

A Toast before Dying
by Grace Yearwood

This is a murder mystery that deals with everyday Harlem life, big-city corruption, and the fear of "other" people, which usually leads to racism.

These and many other storytellers of the era provided hope and a feeling of unity for a community that was feeling under siege.

We have come to reclaim the house of history. We are dedicated to the revision of the role of the African in the world's great civilizations, the contribution of Africa to the achievement of man in the arts and sciences. We shall emphasize what Africa has given to the world, not what it has lost.

— Dr. Ivan Van Sertima

8

The Rant Tape

History is usually told by the conqueror—so it is. So it always will be.

Since ancient times conquerors have burned,

chiseled out, or stolen any history or other documentation that would ennoble the defeated. It is a symbolic act, designed to rewrite history and crush the spirits of the conquered.

Since we will all die someday, the only thing that will live on is our name and deeds . . . our legacy.

Erasure has happened to individuals throughout history in various places at various times, but what happens when an entire race of people have their story erased? What happens when generations of people are consistently defined by their conquerors and accept those definitions because they don't have one to replace them?

Unfortunately, we don't have to wonder about these questions because that has been the state of people of African descent in the so-called "New World" for centuries and the results have been spiritually and psychologically disastrous.

However, the tide of injustice would begin to turn in the late nineteenth century when scholars like George Washington Williams and W.E.B. Dubois began to challenge the Eurocentric version of history that denied Africa as the progenitor of human civilization.

It is because of their dedication to telling the conquered side of world history in their writings that these two men are considered the grandfathers of Afrocentric scholarship.

As previously mentioned, in the early nineties people began to rediscover their books and the host of torchbearers that they inspired, but technology allowed Black people to videotape the new scholars giving their speeches on a variety of subjects pertaining to African and world history.

This was absolutely necessary because Black scholars who disagreed with conventional knowledge were sometimes dismissed as crazy, unqualified, or simplistically labeled as militant.

In other words, they were discredited despite having proven themselves as professionals and holding graduate degrees from some of the most respected universities in the country.

To this day, even Blacks in academia who do not rock the boat are rarely quoted or interviewed in relation to anything except Black topics on the news or in documentaries on the History Channel, Discovery Channel, or the National Geographic Channel.

Black academics who challenge the white supremacist vision of world events are rendered invisible. The excuse for this is the claim that Afrocentric scholars espouse "reverse racism" and should not be heard. Thus, they are forced to the periphery of public discourse where they lecture in community centers, houses of worship, independent organizations, universities, and tour groups that seek them out.

During the conscious era these video lectures became quite popular. They were usually sold at Black bookstores and Afrocentric boutiques but most commonly by people on the street in Harlem, Brooklyn, and other Black communities in America.

My friends and I lovingly referred to them as "rant tapes," and we would make a social event by inviting other people over with food to watch our latest purchases, some lectures lasting for hours.

The tapes provided us with a perspective on so many things we never thought about and even made us aware of linguistic brainwashing such as calling Alexander III of Macedon "The Great" instead of an imperialist murderer or calling the Pilgrims "settlers" or "pioneers" instead of invaders.

Prior to these scholars, many of us hadn't realized how racism was actually built into the language itself.

The hip-hop community was listening and groups like Public Enemy and Brand Nubian sampled respected scholars or mentioned their names in their music.

A formal college degree was not a requirement to gain the respect of the viewer, but personal experience through traveling or years of independent study was.

The race of the scholar was also unimportant.

A tape was popular as long as the scholar's agenda was to debunk commonly accepted "facts" and ideas.

This had its good and bad sides for several reasons: First, it prevented an otherwise knowledgeable person from being accepted by some people used to respecting opinions only from degree holders. Second, an unschooled person may not provide a bibliography or reference for the information they present or how they came up with a particular theory, or they use the forum to vent about discrimination or other injustices without staying focused on the topic at hand.

However, in most cases the lecturer was a degree holder such as Dr. Wade Nobles, Dr. Yosef A. A. ben-Jochannan, Dr. Asa Hilliard, the late Dr. John Henrik Clarke, Dr. Ivan Van Sertima, Dr. Ishakamusa Barashango, Dr. Theophile Obenga, Dr. laila Afrika, Dr. Leonard Jeffries, and Dr. Yaa-Lengi M. Ngemi. Ashra and Merira Kwesi are also very popular and well known for the African history tours to Egypt and Ethiopia they have led for many years.

This list is by no means a representation of all the videos available since there are literally hundreds out there.

For many people who don't have the time or the money to take Africana studies courses, these videos provide a wonderful alternative.

I ain't mad at Snoop. I'm not mad at Master P. I ain't mad at the Hot Boyz. I'm mad when that's all you see. I would be mad if I looked up and all I saw on TV was me or Common or the Roots because I know that ain't the whole deal. The real joy is when you can kick it with everyone. That's what hip-hop is all about. They keep trying to slip the conscious rapper thing on me. I come from Roosevelt projects, man. The ghetto. I drank the same sugar water, ate hard candy. And they try to get me because I'm supposed to be more articulate. I'm supposed to be not like the other Negroes, to get me to say something against my brothers. I'm not going out like that.

—Mos Def

9

Soul Searching

The advent of Afrocentric literature in the early nineties that challenged some of the most sacred beliefs of the Western world caused a number of

African Americans to reexamine the spiritual concepts they had been taught since they were children.

For most this meant the eradication of a Christianity based on Eurocentrism to a more African model that included the use of holy art that depicted a Black Jesus, angels, and saints that were more in line with the biblical description of Christ as having "feet the color of burnt brass as if put in a furnace and hair like lamb's wool."

Others chose a more esoteric form of Christianity after the discovery that numerous ecumenical conferences had been held to edit the Bible in Europe. Instead these Christians did away with the formalities and rituals of the religion because of the perception of it being tainted, and concentrated on the actual deeds of Jesus Christ himself as a guide to living. They focused less on what they felt was an overemphasis on the humble Christ in favor of Christ's antiestablishment/ antioppression work as a revolutionary political activist that ultimately got him killed.

Rastafarianism was also seen by many as a good way to balance their Christian beliefs and Afrocentric worldview because of its emphasis on an Ethiopian holy land and Black Nationalism. This was possible due to the popularization of Rasta philosophy via Bob Marley, Peter Tosh, and other popular Roots Reggae artists and the ever-increasing flow of Caribbean immigrants whom many African Americans lived in close proximity to if not in the same neighborhoods, adding to the cross-pollination of ideological influence.

Islam also became attractive during this time due to the widely publicized militancy of controversial Nation of Islam leader Minister Louis Farrakhan. There are three main reasons for the renewed interest in Islam around this time: One, Farrakhan had organized an extensive prison outreach program since 1984 that reformed many Black men while they were incarcerated; two, many had gained a renewed interest in the history and culture of the Moors (many young people did not distinguish the difference between Orthodox Islam and the Nation of Islam who were unrecognized by many communities of the latter); and three, because of the perception of the strength of Muslims portrayed by contemporary hip-hop groups like Public Enemy.

Others sought out African-based religions that had previously been shunned because of their associations with devil worship and "heathenism."

As a result of books that clearly outlined a pattern of conquest that involved the desecration of a native people's concept of God as a prerequisite to subjugating them, many Blacks decided to do their own research and investigate these religions through African eyes.

This often led to alliances with Latino immigrants from Cuba, Puerto Rico, and other parts of the Caribbean who imported these priesthoods to the United States and shared their knowledge with eager African Americans in search of reconnecting with African theology.

Thousands of people became practitioners of Lukumí and Vodou and some even traveled back to Africa in search of spiritual guidance and initiation. Some joined spiritual groups based on what is known of Kemetic religion and philosophy (Kemet was the original name of "Egypt") such as the Ausar Auset Society and the Nuwabians.

X-Clan was instrumental in bringing the concepts

of African spirituality into hip-hop by referring to the names of Yoruba deities called Orishas and Kemetic deities known as the Neteru. In addition they wore many African cultural symbols such as the ankh and presented them in artwork displayed in their music videos.

You know, it's not the world that was my oppressor, because what the world does to you, if the world does it to you long enough and effectively enough, you begin to do to yourself.

—James Baldwin

10

The Bling Plantation

Hip-hop music and culture is not inherently negative. Nor does it cause violence or any other immoral behavior. Art is always a reflection of the society that produces it, so if there is too much sex, too much violence, too much profanity, too much materialism, too much vanity, or too much mysogny, then the society as a whole probably deserves an overhaul.

It is easy to use nonconscious rap music as a scapegoat for all of society's ills. But since the first recorded rap record did not appear until 1979, the negative label will not hold up under scrutiny. Street gangs, drugs, rape, random violence, theft, and misogyny flourished long before any of the rap artists were born.

Perhaps one thing we need to do is take a look at our studies starting from elementary school. America's founding fathers are called virtuous even though some were slaveholders and others sided with acts of imperialism that negatively affect people of color around the world to this very day. The children have cable and the Internet now. They know when they are being fed a pack of lies that they are then forced to repeat on standardized tests in order to graduate. Many of them are angry. They continue to be angry as they get older.

Therefore, my beef is not with the fact that the

"dark side" exists in hip-hop music. I truly believe that everyone has a right to be heard.

My problem is with the lack of balance in perspectives that exists in the music today. I have a problem with the fact that most of today's rap music either celebrates the gangster or just crass materialism.

A beautiful cultural art form has been manipulated to make us slaves once again, this time donning platinum instead of iron chains.

In the early nineties, there was rap music that exalted the narcissistic gangsta types and their half-naked girls who cavorted in the videos. But that rap music coexisted with that of the conscious rappers. There were bohemian rappers waving peace signs as well as hard-core Black Nationalists, so that music lovers had a choice. You could bypass the gangsta rappers and listen to KRS-One or Arrested Development.

Why are we now stuck in a twilight zone where nothing else exists except blasting guns, spinning rims, and naked rumps?

As a nation we are becoming increasingly obsessed every day with convenience, and most people would rather read a tabloid than curl up with a great piece of literature. The result is that we are sacrificing the arts to the gods of crass commercialism in exchange for the illusion of ease. On the surface this makes perfect sense for the majority of people who are already exhausted from a daily rat race for survival or invested in the pathos of industrialized nations that dictates around-the-clock productivity as the only way to be "useful," but it is the lack of vision of the bigger picture that has and will continue to lead to disaster.

While relevant to everyone, this is especially true for youth of color.

Unlike people of other ethnic backgrounds who are exposed to a multidimensional depiction of themselves, Black children are subjected per diem to a stereotypical definition of who they are and what they should aspire to be, unnamable perceptions regarding gender, and a distorted vision of "reality" that will doom succeeding generations to a plague of ignorance and despair.

We need the conscious rappers to come back in full force. When they reappear, we need to use our dollars to support their art.

The Media, Self-Image, and Manifest Destiny

In the social sciences there is a term called "Manifest Destiny," which means that a person or a people who have been consistently subjected to a certain message will eventually come to embody that message.

Nowhere is this more evident than in the exaltation of thugs, gangsters, and pimps by most fans of mainstream hip-hop.

For ten years we have seen more ass, guns, cars, and jewels than real lyrical writing talent simply because sex, violence, blinging jewelry, and pimped-out cars allegedly move more units than clever, thought-provoking lyrics. That means this generation can't remember hip-hop as anything else but the soundtrack to an anti-intellectual, materialistic, nymphomaniacal lifestyle ideal.

If that wasn't bad enough, we have created our own lawn jockey system to criticize those who protest against the minstrel show that used to be our music by calling them "playa haters" while praising studio outlaws for "keeping it real."

Sadly, these same young men inspire envy in their peers by feigning power via a fake thug, hustler, or pimp image. Devoid of the ability to think analytically due to the "worker bee" mentality produced by the public school system and no encouragement to do so anywhere else, no one stops to ask if a real "thug" would let a makeup artist powder his nose for hours prior to a photo shoot, get his nails and eyebrows done, or wear pastels or an ankle bracelet. Or, if we are the "players" who know how to peep "game," then why do people who don't look like us control every aspect of our cultural product while we get a small percentage in comparison to our labor as we strut around in our flashiest clothes and jewels for our customers?

After reflecting on these questions, it is clear who the real hoes and the real pimps are.

Equally absurd is the honor given to the Mafia, murderers, drug cartels, and other negative characters by rappers naming themselves after them. Thus implying that it is better to get paid and meet your end early than make an honest living at a "square" gig.

The most recognized symbol of this in hip-hop today is the character Tony Montana played by Al Pacino in the movie *Scarface*. His image is everywhere from coats, sweaters, and hats to belt buckles as the ultimate symbol of masculinity. Isn't there a better fictional icon who can embody the principle of manhood than an uneducated, arrogant, hotheaded junkie who lost in the end to someone who was more powerful and better organized? Every time I see some kid thinking he looks tough with this image emblazoned on him, I want to remind him that TONY MONTANA LOST THE BATTLE! THE EDUCATED AND WELL-SPOKEN SOSA WON THE WAR!

But I know that, although Sosa was the victor, he simply wasn't as flamboyant or loud enough to inspire the same kind of adulation that Tony has. Thus, flashy "bling" messages go far beyond mere compressed rocks but have settled into the very psyches of inner city youth.

Vanity is even at the source of the stampede to start clothing lines and more rap labels.

In the twenty-first century Black America has an unprecedented number of millionaires but no one is interested in opening desperately needed schools in our communities. Or how about purchasing farmland and opening a supermarket chain? Or car manufacturing plants? It is so obvious that better things could be done with all this money instead of giving it all back to the system via luxury items in a desperate attempt to purchase self-worth. All of these variables contribute to the manifest destiny of young Black Americans as stupid, aspiring criminals with no desire to do anything but have a good time. That is why it is no coincidence that the stereotypes of inarticulateness, sluggish posture, poor grooming, the insatiable desire to sing and dance all the time, bugged eyes, and sex obsession no longer infuriate us as they did in films like *Birth of a Nation*. Instead we embrace them in our own cinema displaying our self-hate for the world.

So where does the necromaniacal, misogynistic criminal-idolizing of mainstream hip-hop lead? The answer really depends on who is doing the asking.

For white teens it probably means they feel they have a connection to or "understand" Black people better after being invited into virtual reality ghettos for years, but at the end of the day it is just a fad for them. White kids are not investing all of their energy into making a way of life based on what they hear off of these records as their Black and Latino counterparts are. White people who choose to remain on the periphery of American society and participate in any "subculture" always have the option of being welcomed back after a haircut and a shave as demonstrated by all those long-haired hippies of the sixties turned conservative by the eighties. Thus, their freedom to choose will always separate them from being able to fully identify or "be down." For most, the phase will conclude and become a much laughed-at section in the family photo album.

Unfortunately this will not be the case with many men of color who think the thug persona is the only way to earn the respect they so desperately crave. They know they will never be treated on equal footing as a man by society at large because of racism, so maintaining "street cred" becomes of paramount importance in order not to feel completely worthless. This has always been the case, but because the criterion for gaining street credibility is so one-dimensional, there is no room for individual growth and exploration as there was in hip-hop's past.

Hence, the creation of thousands of thugs-in-training who will try and relive the colorful tales told by their heroes to escape rampant poverty and unemployment.

Presently, the Black per capita income is approximately three-fifths that of whites, a frightening statistic considering Africans were considered three-fifths of a human being prior to the revision of the United States Constitution. Thousands of Black and Latino men and boys are ending up in early graves and crowding the prisons trying to even the scales in the only way they know how. The glamorization of dope dealing is leading them straight into the trap set for them by the racist "War on Drugs"—a policy that targets minorities in inner cities despite the fact that the average illicit drug user is white and middle class. Yet still, African Americans and Latinos comprise approximately 70 percent of those convicted for drug felonies and have longer sentences imposed on them.

Making matters worse as the definition of "terrorism" becomes increasingly broader after 9/11, there have been pushes by some politicians to include members of street gangs under antiterrorism laws. The domino effect of this is more broken families and an increased incapability to find gainful employment upon release leading to the necessity to return to criminal activity to survive creating a vicious cycle that ultimately may lead to life imprisonment. Even more tragic is the fact that it costs approximately $25,000 a year to maintain a single prisoner, money that could have been spent to improve the conditions that led most of them to "hustling" in the first place.

America presently holds the highest record for imprisoning its own citizens and it's unimaginable how the numbers will skyrocket even more once the money starts rolling in. In addition, the probability of corruption increases significantly to attain more prisoners or "clients." The Black community must put down a collective foot and demand more variation in the music that our children are exposed to and bring back some of the intellectualism of the past. This may be difficult to do initially because a lot of rap music is consumed by whites in suburbia, and neither artists nor record companies will stop production unless the cash flow ceases. However, this will be a nonissue once everyone learns that Black people consider the proliferation of this particular genre of rap music to be "played out."

Studio Pimps, Players, and the Legacy of Black Female Degradation

The other casualty of thug and pimp mania is the image of the Black woman as an accessory instead of a human being. Like the big cars and pit bulls, our oily bodies shaking in submission has become yet another symbolic penis extender. The presentation of the Black female in today's rap music videos has negatively affected the self-esteem of young Black girls who are subliminally taught that all they are useful for is sex.

As the Beat Goes On

After close examination it is clear for all to see that all of the archetypes of slave personalities are still intact, including those from a few tribes that initially sold their people for personal enrichment. The only difference now is that Black people themselves are keeping the archetypes alive via their African oral tradition.

The proliferation of rappers that exchange their soul for baubles and gadgets reminds me of a scene from one of my favorite movies, *Shaka Zulu*, starring the brilliant actor Henry Cele. In a scene toward the end when Shaka is reflecting in front of a crackling fire on how he allowed his kingdom to be taken away from him by the British, who the Zulus nicknamed "swallows," he begins a devastating dialogue with the victorious English lieutenant who is sitting nearby. Having discovered the answer himself of how the takeover was possible by remembering an old hunting technique for trapping monkeys, he asks his conqueror to say it to him.

He asks the solemn-faced lieutenant, "How do you trap a monkey?"

The lieutenant quietly replies, "With an object, something shiny."

Shaka smiles at his own stupidity and quietly asks him what new shiny object he had brought for him today.

The conversation confirmed that Shaka had exchanged everything his ancestors worked for in exchange for gifts and technology that proved useless in comparison.

Although the story takes place two hundred years ago, it is a sad fact that Black people today are trading the words of the conscious for the shiny, shiny bling.

If I could have convinced more slaves that they were slaves, I could have freed thousands more.

—Harriet Tubman

11

Hip-Hop's Underground Railroad

Today there are a number of hip-hop artists struggling to come out of the mud of gangsterdom and pimpnosis to continue the legacy of their golden-era elders. Only this time the movement toward socially unconscious music isn't mainly centered on the East coast but all over the country. They usually rock the house as underground heroes playing to a mainly white audience. Young people of color either don't know about them or they simply can't identify with their message as they have been inoculated with commercial rap serum for over a decade. But the success of excellent "moderates" such as Common and more recently The Roots and Kanye West gives hope that people may be ready to make a change.

By the year 2000, I had abandoned rap music, tired of hearing the "N" word, "bitch," "drink," "fuck," "gun," "murder," tired of participating (by buying this crap) in the genocide of my own people.

But that year, while I was attending a writers workshop at Michigan State University, I met another young writer named Nnedi. She offered me a ride to the dorms and, as we rode down the tree-lined campus street, she popped in a CD, forwarded to track number twelve, and Dead Prez's "Psychology" came booming out of the speakers. I will never forget the joy I felt as I bounced along in the car.

Rap music used to play a huge role in my life. But, after it became violent, overtly sexist, and lyrically unchallenging, I abandoned it and explored other types of music in search of the depth that I'd lost when the socially conscious era ended. And now this tune called "Psychology" was calling me back to hip-hop.

Nnedi told me that she, too, had given up and stopped buying the music until she discovered an Underground Railroad of rappers who were doing the right thing by making conscious rap records even though they would never make as much money as the gangsta rappers.

I was delighted.

As soon as I got back to New York, I purchased *Let's Get Free* for myself and I must have played it so much that even my next-door neighbor asked me who it was. After that, I found and purchased CDs by Talib Kweli, Mos Def, and the veteran, Paris, who had been around since the golden era. Today, there are even more hidden gems on the scene who, like De La Soul's Trugoy would say, are focused on keeping it right instead of trying to "keep it real." Some of these artists' albums are older, but they are worth purchasing to balance the hip-hop bamboozle and they are fantastic.

Here are some of the new rappers with a conscience:

A-Alikes

I Eat, U Eat is the debut album of Illuminessence aka P. Red and Karaam aka A. Black, two Brooklynites on a mission to bring self-conscious awareness back to the streets. They have a determination to do away with the divide-and-conquer techniques that make resistance against oppression impossible. In the tradition of the late Tupac Shakur, their delivery is hard-core and in-your-face with equally gritty beats that are satisfying. My favorite tracks include "They Wanna Murder Me," a song about unjustified violence perpetuated by the police, and "What's Your Politic?" a song that challenges the listener to construct their own perception of what's going on around them. A-Alikes just needs to eliminate the "N" word from all of their lyrics and they, too, can reach conscious rap greatness.

The Coup

Oakland-based rapper Boots Riley and DJ Pam the Funkstress's album *Pick a Bigger Weapon* is a must-buy. Armed with clever, though-provoking lyrics, and Funkadelic-inspired rhythm and playfulness, it is a definite winner. It is extremely difficult to make hard-core political commentary without sounding heavy or preachy but *The Coup* manages to pull it off without a hitch.

Dead Prez

The unapologetic lyrics of this dynamic duo consisting of M-1 and Stic Man really hit home. Their first album, *Let's Get Free,* addresses a wide range of topics including police brutality, government corruption, inadequacies in public education, and processed "Frankenstein" foods. The beats are fantastic and I love the creative intermissions, especially a character monologue from the revolutionary film *The Spook That Sat by the Door,* and that is saying a lot because I usually hate the clutter that interludes often produce.

Their second album, *Revolutionary But Gangsta,*

was a disappointment. The title was downright confusing and it lacked the Byzantine artistry of their debut. They followed up with *Turn off the Radio: Volumes One* and *Two* shortly after. In *Volume One*, I liked the fact that they used popular beats such as Biggie's classic "Juicy," which was also a song about struggle, and Black Rob's party anthem *Whoa* with its neo-Black-Panther-style lyrics.

Volume Two is better and there is a nice collaboration with Tha Outlawz and Onyx but the downside is its brevity. M-1 also came out with a solo album, *Confidential,* that included some nice tracks with a few '80s-flavored beats and intelligent rhymes. My favorites include "Comrade's Call" and "Love You Can't Borrow."

The Perceptionists

Lyricists Mr. Lif, Akrobatic, and DJ Fakts One comprise a trio of talented young men with an emphasis on social commentary, creative sampling, and infectious beats. Their hooks are catchy but clever and go far beyond "desperate for a hit" corniness. They also include tracks with reggae and club influences that give it versatility and depth. My favorite singles are "Blo," "Black Dialogue," and "People 4 Prez." Whether they are discussing the Bush administration or exploring the triumphs and tragedies of everyday life, it is clear that they are not boardroom-conceived MCs.

Zion-1

MC Zion and DJ Amp Live provide a refreshing break from assembly-line rap with danceable but intelligent lyrics. A far cry from simplistic refried sampling techniques, DJ Amp Live showcases classic mixing techniques while MC Zion offers a smooth, laid-back flow with real storytelling capabilities. Their latest album, *True and Livin',* is genius with intro and outro by Fred Hampton Jr. (son of slain Black Panther Fred Hampton) and beautiful tracks like "Bird's Eye View" and "What U Hear." The album also includes other talented artists such as Del the Funky Homosapien, Aesop Rock, and one of my favorites, Talib Kweli. Their mix tapes and full-length albums are also a must-have in any conscious hip-hop collection.

> If you allow men to use you for your own purposes, they will use you for theirs.

> —Aesop

12

The Illusion of Inclusion and the Death of Hip-Hop Poets

People of African descent all over the world are the most despised, the most feared, the most misunderstood, and the most blamed people for societies' ills, but we are also the most copied group on the planet.

Our music. How we dance. How we wear our hair. How we speak. How we dress. The way we move. It has always been seen as the epitome of cool.

Although Blacks usually set the standard for what is hot, rarely do we end up profiting in the long run from our own genius. Whether it is inventions like the refrigerator or air conditioner or peanut butter, eventually we are always sold out and everyone forgets the Black originators.

I predict the same fate for hip-hop if the community continues to collectively stick its head in the sand without addressing the continued threat posed by cultural imperialism and doing something about it.

Multiculturalism versus Cultural Colonialism

Since I was a child, I have always had a fondness for researching other cultures. I would flip through countless photo books, encyclopedias, and magazines that documented the human experience in all of its rich diversity. I fantasized about trips around the world where I would taste different cuisine, learn new languages, admire art, appreciate landscapes, and visit sacred ruins and temples to admire humanity's accomplishments. I think it is absolutely essential to read about world-views other than one's own.

Living in close proximity to different cultures is not enough to gain understanding, either, because if that were the case there would be a dialogue between various racial and ethnic groups in all of the major cities in the country. The truth is, we only want superficial multiculturalism: Yoga at our local gym, tattoos with Chinese characters, burritos or "wraps" from the store on the corner.

True multiculturalism is only possible when the cultures attempting to unite have a real knowledge of and respect for each other, not when one is seen as a convenient commodity or objectified as an exotic "other."

For African Americans who already suffer from identity crisis due to the fact that we were stripped of our African heritage and we have never been fully accepted here, the usurpation of what identity we have managed to piece together has damaged us even further. While other racial and ethnic groups can always reembrace their native languages and ways of life when they have finished experimenting, we are the only race that cannot. It is for this reason that people of African descent around the world must be even more vigilant at maintaining what they have. That includes our beloved spoken-word traditions and hip-hop.

Who's Your Daddy?

Rap music was born in the slums of the Bronx and has traveled around the world. Its beat is heard from Bangladesh to Beverly Hills and everyone is moving to it. This cross-pollination wouldn't have been possible, though, without the backing of very powerful people and music companies with the means and the will to do so. Although the spread and celebration of hip-hop worldwide is a positive thing, the exploitation of the people who created it is not.

In 1989, DJ Jazzy Jeff and the Fresh Prince were the first to win Best Rap Performance at the Grammy Awards. The duo boycotted the event because they were only scheduled as part of the preshow ceremony, not the main and televised event.

It was almost a decade later that the Grammy

folks included rap in the general music categories of Album of the Year and Record of the Year. By this time most rap music was under corporate control. These corporations were not going to stand for the exclusion of its investments from one of the most internationally watched awards shows in the world.

Today, rap music is like a double-stuffed Oreo cookie with many Blacks acting as figureheads for a white governing body that ultimately owns everything. In fact, the publishing rights to most American rap music are European controlled via EMI Group (England), Vivendi-Universal (France), and Bertelsmann AG (Germany). Viacom and Time Warner Inc. are also conglomerates that have their hands in the ghetto cookie jar but they are both based in New York City.

Worse, the majority of hip-hop trade and fan magazines are owned by people who are not Black and, even scarier, most of the staff members aren't, either. It is scary because these publications create and define hip-hop culture on a monthly basis. The whole scheme smacks of colonial policy that traditionally extracted the natural resources of the subjugated country (hip-hop being the "resource" and African Americans the "country"), refined it in the colonial motherland (or in this case the corporation), and sold the finished product back to the natives.

Futuristic Hip-Hop

The year is 2047 and there is a rap concert advertised in the paper at an upscale venue located in the poshest neighborhood in your local town. The show will feature mostly Caucasian rappers with a few Blacks (only if they have been schooled at a prestigious music conservatory and majored in Hip–Hop Studies) thrown in.

The ticket for this event is way over $200 but your grandchildren have saved up enough money to take you there as a birthday present. Your grandchildren have heard that an old-timer named Busta Rhymes is the guest of honor and that you loved the old geezer in your youth.

Your eyes mist with gratitude. As you ride to the event, you chatter incessantly about the good ole days when rap music and clubs were located in the Black community. Your grandchildren roll their eyes, wishing you would stop talking about a musical genre that they do not respect at all.

You remember that your children didn't care for it, either. They felt it had become irrelevant to Black life and culture a long time ago. Your shoulders slump in defeat because they are right.

It happened to jazz.

It is happening to rap music.

Right now.

Recommended Reading

Chang, Jeff. *Can't Stop Won't Stop*. New York: St. Martin's Press, 2005.

Chuck D. *Public Enemy*. New York: Thunder's Mouth Press, 1994.

George, Nelson. *Hip Hop America*. New York: Penguin Books, 2005.

Kool Mo Dee. *There's a God on the Mic*. New York: Thunder's Mouth Press, 2003.

Lee, Spike. *That's My Story and I'm Sticking to It*. New York: W. W. Norton & Company, 2005.

Queen Latifah. *Ladies First: Revelations of a Strong Woman*. New York: William Morrow, 1999.

Souljah, Sister. *The Coldest Winter Ever*. New York: Simon & Schuster/Atria, 2004.

Vibe Magazine. *The Vibe History of Hip Hop*. New York: Three Rivers Press, 1999.

Watkins, S. Craig. *Hip Hop Matters*. Boston: Beacon Press, 2006.

Recommended Listening

ARRESTED DEVELOPMENT
3 Years, 5 Months & 2 Days in the Life Of . . .
Chrysalis Records

Arrested Development Unplugged
EMI Records

Zingalamaduni
Capitol Records

Da Feelin' EP
EMI records

Heroes of the Harvest (Import)
Vagabond

Among the Trees (Import)
Edel Records

Since the Last Time (Import)
Wagram Records

BRAND NUBIAN
One for All
Elektra Records

In God We Trust
Elektra Records

Everything is Everything
Elektra Records

Foundation
Arista Records

Fire in the Hold
Babygrande Records

DE LA SOUL
3 Feet High and Rising
Tommy Boy Records

De La Soul is Dead
Tommy Boy Records

Buhloone Mindstate
Tommy Boy Records

Clear Lake Audiotorium EP
Tommy Boy Records

Stakes is High
Tommy Boy Records

Live at Tramps, NYC, 1996
Rhino Entertainment

Art Official Intelligence: Mosaic Thump
Tommy Boy Records

AOI: Bionix
Tommy Boy Records

Timeless: The Singles Collection
Rhino Records

The Grind Date
Sanctuary Records

ERIC B. & RAKIM
Paid in Full
Zakia/ 4th & Broadway

Follow the Leader
Uni Records

Let the Rhythm Hit 'Em
MCA

Don't Sweat the Technique
MCA

Gold
Hip-O Records

GANGSTARR
No More Mr. Nice Guy
Wild Pitch

Step in the Arena
Chrysalis Records

Daily Operation
Chrysalis Records

Hard to Earn
Chrysalis Records

Moment of Truth
Noo Trybe Records

Full Clip: A Decade of Gangstarr
Cooltempo/Virgin Records

The Ownerz
Virgin Records

GRANDMASTER FLASH & THE FURIOUS FIVE
The Message
Sugar Hill Records

They Said It Couldn't Be Done
Elektra Records

The Source
Elektra Records

Ba-Dop-Boom-Bang
Elektra Records

On the Strength
Elektra Records

Salsoul Jam 2000
Salsoul Records

The Official Adventures of Grandmaster Flash
Strut Records

Essential Mix: Classic Edition
Strut Records

Mixing Bullets and Firing Joints
Salsoul UK

ICE CUBE
AmeriKKKa's Most Wanted
Priority Records

Kill at Will
Priority Records

Death Certificate
Priority Records

The Predator
Priority Records

Lethal Injection
Priority Records

War & Peace—Volume 1 (The War Disc)
Priority Records

War & Peace—Volume 2 (The Peace Disc)
Priority Records

Greatest Hits
Priority Records

Laugh Now, Cry Later
Lench Mob Records

NAS
Illmatic
Columbia Records

It Was Written
Columbia Records

Nastradamas
Columbia Records

Stillmatic
Columbia Records

PUBLIC ENEMY
Yo! Bum Rush the Show
Def Jam/Columbia Records

*It Takes a Nation of Millions
to Hold Us Back*
Def Jam/Columbia Records

Fear of a Black Planet
Def Jam/Columbia Records

Apocalypse '91 . . . The Enemy Strikes Back
Def Jam/Columbia Records

Greatest Misses
Def Jam/Columbia Records

Muse Sick-n-Hour Mess Age
Def Jam

There's a Poison Goin' On
Play It Again Sam/Atomic Pop

Revolverlution
Kock Records

New Whirl Odor
Slam Jamz

Power to the People and the Beats:
Public Enemy's Greatest Hits
Def Jam

Rebirth of a Nation
Guerrilla Funk/Groove Attack

QUEEN LATIFAH
All Hail the Queen
Tommy Boy

Nature of a Sista
Tommy Boy

Black Reign
Motown

Order in the Court
Motown

She's the Queen: A Collection of Hits
Motown

The Dana Owens Album
Interscope Records

X-CLAN
To the East, Blackwards
4th & Broadway/Island/PolyGram Records

Xodus
PolyGram Records

Return from Mecca
Suburban Noize Records

YZ
Sons of the Father
Tuff City Records

EP
Tuff City Records

The Ghetto's Been Good to Me
Livin' Large Records

Legend of Floyd Jones
Select-O-Hits, Inc.

The Best of YZ
Tuff City Records

Recommended Viewing

Boyz n the Hood
Laurence Fishburne, Cuba Gooding Jr., Ice Cube, Morris Chestnut, Nia Long, Angela Bassett, Tyra Ferrell, Lexie Bigham, Hudhail Al-Amir, Lloyd Avery II, Mia Bell, Kenneth A. Brown, Nicole Brown, Ceal, Desi Arnez Hines II
Columbia Pictures
Producer: Steve Nicolaides
Director: John Singleton
Screenplay: John Singleton
Cinematography: Charles Mills
107 minutes. Color.

Daughters of the Dust

Cora Lee Day, Alva Rogers, Barbarao, Trula Hoosier, Umar Abdurrahamn, Adisa Anderson, Kaycee Moore, Bahni Turpin, Cheryl Lynn Bruce, Tommy Redmond Hicks, Malik Farrakhan, Cornell Royal, Vertamae Grosvenor, Sherry Jackson, Reverend Ervin Green
Kino International Corp.
Producers: Julie Dash, Pamm R. Jackson, Arthur Jafa, Steven Jones, Lindsay Law, Bernard Nicolas, Floyd Webb
Director: Julie Dash
Screenplay: Julie Dash
Cinematography: Arthur Jafa
112 minutes. Color.

Do the Right Thing

Ossie Davis, Danny Aiello, Giancarlo Esposito, Richard Edson, Spike Lee, Ruby Dee, Bill Nunn, John Turturro, Paul Benjamin, Rosie Perez, Robin Harris, Frankie Faison, Steve White, Leonard L. Thomas, Samuel L. Jackson
MCA/Universal Pictures
Producers: John Kilik, Spike Lee, Monty Ross

Director: Spike Lee
Screenplay: Spike Lee
Cinematography: Ernest R. Dickerson
120 minutes. Color.

Get on the Bus
Richard Belzer, De'aundre Bonds, Andre Braugher, Thomas Jefferson Byrd, Gabriel Casseus, Albert Hall, Hill Harper, Harry J. Lennix, Bernie Mac, Wendell Pierce, Roger Guenveur Smith, Isaiah Washington, Steve White, Ossie Davis, Charles S. Dutton
Columbia Pictures
Producers: Bill Borden, Reuben Cannon, Spike Lee, Barry Rosenbush
Director: Spike Lee
Screenplay: Reggie Rock Bythewood
Cinematography: Elliot Davis
120 minutes. Color.

Hollywood Shuffle
Robert Townsend, Craigus R. Johnson, Helin Martin, Starletta DuPois, Marc Figueroa, Sarah Kaite Coughlan, Sean Michael Flynn, Brad Sanders, David

McKnight, Keenen Ivory Wayans, Lou B. Washington, Anne-Marie Johnson, Don Reed, Kim Wayans, Gregory "Popeye" Alexander
Samuel Goldwyn Company
Producers: Carl Craig, Richard Cummings Jr., Robert Townsend
Director: Robert Townsend
Screenplay: Robert Townsend, Keenen Ivory Wayans
Cinematography: Peter Deming
78 minutes. Color.

Jungle Fever
Wesley Snipes, Annabella Sciorra, Spike Lee, Ossie Davis, Ruby Dee, Samuel L. Jackson, Lonette McKee, John Turturro, Frank Vincent, Anthony Quinn, Halle Berry, Tyra Ferrell, Veronica Webb, Veronica Timbers, David Dundara
Universal Pictures
Producers: John Kilik, Spike Lee, Monty Ross
Director: Spike Lee
Screenplay: Spike Lee
Cinematography: Ernest R. Dickerson
132 minutes. Color.

Malcolm X

Denzel Washington, Angela Bassett, Albert Hall, Al Freeman Jr., Delroy Lindo, Spike Lee, Theresa Randle, Kate Vernon, Lonette McKee, Tommy Hollis, James McDaniel, Ernest Thomas, Jean-Claude La Marre, O.L. Duke, Larry McCoy

Warner Bros. Pictures

Producers: Preston L. Holmes, Jon Kilik, Spike Lee, Ahmed Murad, Monty Ross, Fernando Sulichin, Marvin Worth

Director: Spike Lee

Screenplay: Arnold Perl, Spike Lee (based on the book *The Autobiography of Malcolm X* by Alex Haley and Malcolm X)

Cinematography: Ernest R. Dickerson

202 minutes. Color.

Sankofa

Kofi Ghanaba, Oyafunmike Ogunlano, Alexandra Duah, Nick Medley, Mutabaruka, Afemo Omilami, Reggie Carter, Mzuri, Jimmy Lee Savage, Hasinatu Camara, Jim Faircloth, Stanley Michelson, John A. Mason, Louise Reid, Roger Doctor

Mypheduh Films
Producers: Shirikiana Aina, Ada Marie Babino, Haile Gerima
Director: Haile Gerima
Screenplay: Haile Gerima
Cinematography: Augustin Cubano
125 minutes. Color.

School Daze

Laurence Fishburne, Giancarlo Esposito, Tisha Campbell, Kyme, Joe Seneca, Ellen Holly, Art Evans, Ossie Davis, Bill Nunn, James Bond III, Branford Marsalis, Kadeem Hardison, Eric Payne, Spike Lee, Anthony Thompkins
Columbia Pictures
Producers: Grace Blake, Loretha C. Jones, Spike Lee, Monty Ross
Director: Spike Lee
Screenplay: Spike Lee
Cinematography: Ernest R. Dickerson
121 minutes. Color.